Hugh Clifford

In Court & Kampong

Being Tales & Sketches of Native Life in the Malay Peninsula

Hugh Clifford

In Court & Kampong
Being Tales & Sketches of Native Life in the Malay Peninsula

ISBN/EAN: 9783337018948

Printed in Europe, USA, Canada, Australia, Japan

Cover: Foto ©ninafisch / pixelio.de

More available books at **www.hansebooks.com**

IN
COURT & KAMPONG

BEING

TALES & SKETCHES OF NATIVE LIFE
IN THE MALAY PENINSULA

BY

HUGH CLIFFORD

London
GRANT RICHARDS
48 LEICESTER SQUARE

To My Wife

My knowledge of all these things was won
   Ere to gladden my life You came,
But the Land I knew, the Deeds saw done
   Will be never again the same,
For You have come, like the rising Sun,
   To golden my World with your flame.

H. C.

PREFACE

The nineteen tales and sketches, which are enclosed within the covers of this Book, relate to certain brown men and obscure things in a distant and very little known corner of the Earth. The Malay Peninsula —that slender tongue of land which projects into the tepid seas at the extreme south of the Asiatic Continent —is but little more than a name to most dwellers in Europe. But, even in the Peninsula itself, and to the majority of those white men whose whole lives have been passed in the Straits of Malacca, the East Coast and the remote interior, of which I chiefly write, are almost as completely unknown.

It has been my endeavour, in writing this book, to give some idea of the lives lived in these lands by Europeans whose lot has led them away from the beaten track; by the aboriginal tribes of *Sâkai* and *Sèmang;* but, above all, by those Malays who, being yet untouched by contact with white men, are still in a state of original sin. My stories deal with natives of all classes; dwellers in the Courts of Kings; peasants in their *kampongs,* or villages, by the rivers and the rice-fields; and with the fisher-folk on the seashore. I have tried to describe these things as they appear when viewed from the inside, as I have myself seen them during the many dreary years that I have spent in the wilder parts of the Malay Peninsula. It will be found that the pictures thus drawn are not always attractive—what man's life, when viewed from the inside, ever is pretty to look at? But I have told my tales of these curious companions of my exile, nothing extenuating, but setting down nought in malice.

The conditions of life of which I write, more especially in those sketches and tales which deal with native society in an Independent Malay State, are rapidly passing away. Nor can this furnish matter for regret to any one who knew them as they were and still are in some of the wilder and more remote regions of the Peninsula. One may, perhaps, feel some measure of sentimental sorrow that the natural should here, as elsewhere, be replaced by the artificial; one may recognise with sufficient clearness that the Malay in his natural unregenerate state is more attractive an individual than he is apt to become under the influence of European civilisation; but no one who has seen the horrors of native rule, and the misery to which the people living under it are ofttimes reduced, can find room to doubt that, its many drawbacks notwithstanding, the only salvation for the Malays lies in the increase of British influence in the

Peninsula, and in the consequent spread of modern ideas, progress, and civilisation.

I feel this so strongly that, in common with many of my countrymen, I am content to devote the best years of my life to an attempt to bring about some of those revolutions in facts and in ideas which we hold to be for the ultimate good of the race. None the less, however, this book has been written in a spirit of the deepest sympathy with all classes of Malays, and I have striven throughout to appreciate the native point of view, and to judge the people and their actions by their own standards, rather than by those of a White Man living in their midst.

With regard to the tales themselves, many of them have been told to me by natives, and all are more or less founded on fact. Some of the incidents related have come under my personal observation, and for the truth of these I can vouch. For the accuracy of the remaining stories others are responsible, and I can only be held answerable for the framing of the pictures.

HUGH CLIFFORD.

BRITISH RESIDENCY,
PAHANG, MALAY PENINSULA,
November 7, 1896.

CONTENTS

As I came through the Desert thus it was,
As I came through the Desert.
The City of Dreadful Night.

		PAGE
1.	THE EAST COAST	1
2.	THE PEOPLE OF THE EAST COAST	17
3.	THE EXPERIENCES OF RÂJA HAJI HAMID	30
4.	THE BATTLE OF THE WOMEN	37
5.	IN COCK-PIT AND BULL-RING	46
6.	THE WERE-TIGER	62
7.	THE ÂMOK OF DÂTO KÂYA BÎJI DĔRJA	78
8.	THE FLIGHT OF CHÊP THE BIRD	96
9.	THE VAULTING AMBITION	111
10.	'ONE MORE UNFORTUNATE'	125
11.	AMONG THE FISHER-FOLK	134
12.	THE STORY OF BÂYAN THE PAROQUET	151
13.	THE TALE OF A THEFT	161
14.	IN A CAMP OF THE SĔMANGS	171
15.	HIS HEART'S DESIRE	182
16.	A NIGHT OF TERROR	196
17.	IN THE DAYS WHEN THE LAND WAS FREE	210
18.	UN MAUVAIS QUART D'HEURE	230
19.	UP COUNTRY	245

L'ENVOI

THE EAST COAST

> The charmed sunset linger'd low adown
> In the red West : thro' mountain clefts the dale
> Was seen far inland, and the yellow down
> Border'd with palm, and many a winding vale
> And meadow, set with slender galingale ;
> A land where all things always seem'd the same !
> And round about the keel with faces pale,
> Dark faces pale against that rosy flame,
> The mild-eyed melancholy Lotos-eaters came.
> *The Lotos-Eaters.*

IN these days, the boot of the ubiquitous white man leaves its marks on all the fair places of the Earth, and scores thereon an even more gigantic track than that which affrighted Robinson Crusoe in his solitude. It crushes down the forests, beats out roads, strides across the rivers, kicks down native institutions, and generally tramples on the growths of nature, and the works of primitive man, reducing all things to that dead level of conventionality, which we call civilisation. Incidentally, it stamps out much of what is best in the customs and characteristics of the native races against which it brushes ; and, though it relieves them of many things which hurt and oppressed them ere it came, it injures them morally almost as much as it benefits them materially. We, who are white men, admire our work not a little—which is natural—and many are found willing to wear out their souls in efforts to clothe in the stiff garments of European conventionalities, the naked, brown limbs of Orientalism. The natives, who, for the most part, are frank Vandals, also admire efforts of which they are aware that they are themselves incapable, and even the *laudator temporis acti* has his mouth stopped by the cheap and often tawdry luxury, which the coming of the Europeans has placed within his reach. So effectually has the heel of the white man been ground into the face of Pêrak and Sĕlângor, that these Native States are now only nominally what their name implies. The alien population far out-numbers the people of the land in most of the principal districts, and it is possible for a European to spend weeks in either of these States without coming into contact with any Asiatics save those who wait at table, wash his shirts, or drive his cab. It is also possible, I am told, for a European to spend years on the West Coast of the Peninsula without acquiring any very profound knowledge of the natives of the country, or of the language which is their speech-medium. This being so, most of the white men who live in the Protected Native States are somewhat apt to disregard the effect which their actions have upon the natives, and labour under the common European inability to view matters from the native standpoint. Moreover, we have become accustomed to existing conditions, and thus it is that few, perhaps, realise the precise nature of the work which the British in the Peninsula have set themselves to accomplish. What we are really attempting, however, is nothing less than to crush into twenty years the revolutions in facts and in ideas which, even in energetic Europe, six long centuries have been needed to accomplish. No one will, of course, be found to dispute that the strides made in our knowledge of the art of government, since the Thirteenth Century, are prodigious and vast, nor that the general condition of the people of Europe has been immensely improved since that day; but, nevertheless, one cannot but sympathise with the Malays, who are suddenly and violently translated from the point to which they had attained in the natural development of their race, and are required to live up to the standards of a people who are six centuries in advance of them in national progress. If a plant is made to blossom or bear fruit three months before its time, it is regarded as a triumph of the gardener's art; but what, then, are we to say of this huge moral-forcing system which we call 'Protection'? Forced plants, we know, suffer in the process; and the Malay, whose proper place is amidst the conditions of the Thirteenth Century, is apt to become morally week and seedy, and to lose something of his robust self-respect, when he is forced to bear Nineteenth-Century fruit.

Until the British Government interfered in the administration of the Malay States in 1874, the people of the Peninsula were, to all intents and purposes, living in the Middle Ages. Each State was ruled by its own Sultàn or *Râja* under a complete Feudal System, which presents a curiously close parallel to that which was in force in Mediæval Europe. The *Râja* was, of course, the paramount authority, and all power emanated from him. Technically, the whole country was his property, and all its inhabitants his slaves; but each State was divided into districts which were held in fief by the *Ôrang Bĕsar*, or Great Chiefs. The conditions on which these fiefs were held, were homage, and military and other service. The Officers were hereditary, but succession was subject to the sanction of the *Râja*, who personally invested and ennobled each Chief, and gave him, as an ostensible sign of authority, a warrant and a State spear, both of which were returned to the *Râja* on the death of the holder. As in Europe, high treason (*dĕrhâka*) was the only offence which warranted the *Râja* in forfeiting a fief. Each of the districts was sub-divided into minor baronies, which were held, on a similar tenure, from the District Chief by a *Dâtô' Mûda;* and the village communes, of which these baronies were composed, were held in a like manner, and on similar conditions, by the Headmen from the *Dâtô' Mûda*. When war or any other public work was toward, the *Râja* summoned the Great Chiefs, who transmitted the order to their *Dâtô' Mûda*. By the latter, the village Headmen and their able-bodied *räayat*[1] were called together, the free-holders in each village being bound to the local *Pĕnghûlu*[2] by ties similar to those which bound him to his immediate Chief. In the same way, the *Râja* made his demands for money-grants to the Great

---

[1] *Räayat* = Peasants, villagers.
[2] *Pĕnghûlu* = Headman.

Chiefs, and the *raäyat* supplied the necessary contributions, while their superiors gained the credit attaching to those who fulfil the desires of the King. Under this system, the *raäyat*, of course, possessed no rights, either of person or property. He was entirely in the hands of the Chiefs, was forced to labour unremittingly that others might profit by his toil; and neither his life, his land, his cattle, nor the very persons of his women-folk, could properly be said to belong to him, since all were at the mercy of any one who desired to take them from him, and was strong enough to do so. This, of course, is the weak point in the Feudal System, and was probably not confined to the peoples of Asia. The chroniclers of Mediæval Europe tell only of Princes and Nobles, and Knights and Dames —and merry tales they are—but we are left to guess what was the condition of the bulk of the lower classes in Thirteenth-Century England. If we knew all, however, it is probable that their lot would prove to have been but little more fortunate than is that of the Malay *raäyat* of to-day, whose hardships and grievances, under native rule, move our modern souls to indignation and compassion. Therefore, we should be cautious how we apply our *fin de siècle* standards to a people whose ideas of the fitness of things are much the same as those which prevailed in Europe some six centuries agone.

Those who love to indulge in that pleasing but singularly useless pastime of imagining what might have been under certain impossible circumstances, will find occupation in speculating as to whether the Malays, had they remained free from all extraneous influence for another thousand years, would ever have succeeded in evolving a system of Government in any way resembling our own, out of a Feudal System which presents so curious a parallel to that from which our modern institutions have sprung. Would the Great Chiefs have ever combined to wrest a Magna Charta from an unwilling King, and the *raäyat* have succeeded in beating down the tyranny of their Chiefs? No answer can be given; but those who know the Malays best will find reason to doubt whether the energy of the race would ever, under any circumstances, have been sufficient to grapple with these great questions. The *raäyat* would have been content, I fancy, to plod on through the centuries 'without hope of change'; and, so far as the past history of a people can be taken as giving an indication of its future, it would seem that, in Malay countries, the growing tendencies made rather for an absolute than for a limited monarchy. The genius of the Malay is in most things mimetic rather than original, and, where he has no other model at hand to copy, he falls back upon the past. An observer of Malay political tendencies in an Independent Native State finds himself placed in the position of Inspector Bucket—there is no move on the board which would surprise him, provided that it is in the wrong direction.

Such changes have been wrought in the condition of the Malay on the West Coast, during the past twenty years of British Protection, that there one can no longer see him in his natural and unregenerate state. He has become sadly dull, limp, and civilised.

The gossip of the Court, and the tales of ill things done daringly, which delighted his fathers, can scarcely quicken his slackened pulses. His wooings have lost their spice of danger, and, with it, more than half their romance. He is as frankly profligate as his thin blood permits, but the dissipation in which he indulges only makes him a disreputable member of society, and calls for none of the manly virtues which make the Malay attractive to those who know and love him in his truculent untamed state. On the East Coast, things are different, and the Malay States are still what they profess to be—States in which the native element predominates, where the people still think boldly from right to left, and lead much the same lives as those their forbears led before them. Here are still to be found some of the few remaining places, on this over-handled Earth, which have as yet been but little disturbed by extraneous influences, and here the lover of things as they are, and ought not to be, may find a dwelling among an unregenerate and more or less uncivilised people, whose customs are still unsullied by European vulgarity, and the surface of whose lives is but little ruffled by the fever-heated breath of European progress.

As you crush your way out of the crowded roadstead of Singapore, and skirting the red cliffs of Tânah Mêrah, slip round the heel of the Peninsula, you turn your back for a space on the seas in which ships jostle one another, and betake yourself to a corner of the globe where the world is very old, and where conditions of life have seen but little change during the last thousand years. The only modern innovation is an occasional 'caster,' or sea tramp, plying its way up the coast to pick up a precarious profit for its owners by carrying cargoes of evil-smelling trade from the fishing villages along the shore. Save for this, there is nothing to show that white men ever visit these seas, and, sailing up the coast in a native craft, you may almost fancy yourself one of the early explorers skirting the lovely shores of some undiscovered country. As you sprawl on the bamboo decking under the shadow of the immense palm leaf sail—which is so ingeniously rigged that, if taken aback, the boat must turn turtle, unless, by the blessing of the gods, the mast parts asunder—you look out through half-closed eyelids at a very beautiful coast. The waves dance, and glimmer, and shine in the sunlight, the long stretch of sand is yellow as a buttercup, and the fringes of graceful *casuarina* trees quiver like aspens in the breeze, and shimmer in the heat haze. The wash of the waves against the boat's side, and the ripple of the bow make music in your drowsy ears, and, as you glide through cluster after cluster of thickly-wooded islands, you lie in that delightful comatose state in which you have all the pleasure of existence with none of the labour of living. The monsoon threshes across these seas for four months in the year, and keeps them fresh, and free from the dingy mangrove clumps, and hideous banks of mud, which breed fever and mosquitoes in the Straits of Malacca. In the interior, too, patches of open country abound, such as are but rarely met with on the West Coast, but here, as elsewhere in the Peninsula, the jungles, which shut down around them, are impenetrable to anything less persuasive than an axe.

These forests are among the wonderful things of the Earth. They are immense in extent, and the trees which form them grow so close together that they tread on one another's toes. All are lashed, and bound, and relashed, into one huge magnificent tangled net, by the thickest underwood, and the most marvellous parasitic growths that nature has ever devised. No human being can force his way through this maze of trees, and shrubs, and thorns, and plants, and creepers; and even the great beasts which dwell in the jungle find their strength unequal to the task, and have to follow game paths, beaten out by the passage of innumerable animals, through the thickest and deepest parts of the forest. The branches cross and recross, and are bound together by countless parasitic creepers, forming a green canopy overhead, through which the fierce sunlight only forces a partial passage, the struggling rays flecking the trees on which they fall with little splashes of light and colour. The air 'hangs heavy as remembered sin,' and the gloom of a great cathedral is on every side. Everything is damp, and moist, and oppressive. The soil, and the cool dead leaves under foot are dank with decay, and sodden to the touch. Enormous fungous growths flourish luxuriantly; and over all, during the long hot hours of the day, hangs a silence as of the grave. Though these jungles teem with life, no living thing is to be seen, save the busy ants, a few brilliantly-coloured butterflies and insects, and an occasional nest of bees high up in the tree-tops. A little stream ripples its way over the pebbles of its bed, and makes a humming murmur in the distance; a faint breeze sweeping over the forest gently sways the upper branches of a few of the tallest trees; but, for the rest, all is melancholy, silent, and motionless. As the hour of sunset approaches, the tree beetles and cicada join in their strident chorus, which tells of the dying day; the thrushes join in the song with rich trills and grace-notes; the jungle fowls crow to one another; the monkeys whoop and give tongue like a pack of fox-hounds; the gaudy parrots scream and flash as they hunt for flies;

> And all the long-pent stream of life
> Bursts downwards in a cataract.

Then, as you lie listening through the long watches of the night, sounds are borne to you which tell that the jungle is afoot. The argus pheasants yell to one another as the hours creep by; the far-away trumpet of an elephant breaks the stillness; and the frightened barking cry of a deer comes to you from across the river. The insects are awake all night, and the little workman bird sits on a tree close by you and drives coffin nails without number. With the dawn, the tree beetles again raise their chorus; the birds sing and trill more sweetly than in the evening; the monkeys bark afresh as they leap through the branches; and the leaves of the forest glisten in the undried dew. Then, as the sun mounts, and the dew dries, the sounds of the jungle die down one by one, until the silence of the forest is once more unbroken for the long hot day.

Through these jungles innumerable streams and rivers flow seawards; for so marvellously is this country watered that, from end to end of the Peninsula, no two hills are found, but there is a stream of some sort in the gut which divides them. Far up-country, the rivers run riot through long successions of falls and rapids, but as they near the coast, they settle down into broad imposing looking streams, miles wide in places, but for the most part uniformly shallow, the surfaces of which are studded with green islands and yellow sandbanks. These rivers, on the East Coast, form the principal, and often the only highways, many of them being navigated for nearly three hundred miles of their course. When they become too much obstructed by falls to be navigable even for a dug-out, they still serve the Malays of the interior as highways. Where they are very shallow indeed they are used as tracks, men wading up them for miles and miles. A river-bed is a path ready cleared through the forests, and, to the Sĕmang,[1] Sâkai,[2] and jungle-bred Malay, it is Nature's macadamized road. More often the unnavigable streams serve as guides to the traveller in the dense jungles, the tracks running up their banks, crossing and recrossing them at frequent intervals. One of these paths, which leads from Trĕnggânu to Kĕlantan, crosses the same river no less than thirty times in about six miles, and, in most places, the fords are well above a tall man's knee. The stream is followed until a *ka-naik*—or taking-off place—is reached, and, leaving it, the traveller crosses a low

---

[1] *Sĕmang* = Aboriginal natives of the Peninsula, belonging to the Negrit family.

[2] *Sâkai* = Aboriginal natives of the Peninsula, belonging to the Mon-Annam family.

range of hills, and presently strikes the banks of a stream, which belongs to another river basin. A path, similar to the one which he has just left, leads down this stream, and by following it he will eventually reach inhabited country. No man need ever lose himself in a Malay jungle. He can never have any difficulty in finding running water, and this, if followed down, means a river, and a river presupposes a village sooner or later. In the same way, a knowledge of the localities in which the rivers of a country rise, and a rough idea of the directions in which they flow, are all the geographical data which are required in order to enable you to find your way, unaided, into any portion of that, or the adjoining States which you may desire to visit. This is the secret of travelling through Malay jungles, in places where the white man's roads are still far to seek, and where the natives are content to move slowly, as their fathers did before them.

The Malay States on the East of the Peninsula are Sĕnggôra, Pĕtâni, Jambe, Jâring, Râman, Lĕgeh, Kĕlantan, Trĕnggânu, Pahang, and Johor.

Sĕnggôra possesses the doubtful privilege of being ruled by a Siamese Official, who is appointed from Bangkok, as the phrase goes, to *kin*—or eat—the surrounding district.

The next four States are usually spoken of collectively as Pĕtâni, by Europeans, though the territory which really bears that name is of insignificant importance and area, the jurisdiction of its *Râja* only extending up the Pĕtâni river as far as Jambe. It is said that when the Râja of Pĕtâni and the ruler of the latter State had a difference of opinion, the former was obliged to send to Kĕlantan for his drinking water, since he could not trust his neighbour to refrain from poisoning the supply, which flows from Jambe through his kingdom. Uneasy indeed must lie the head which wears the crown of Pĕtâni!

All the States, as far down the coast as Lĕgeh, are under the protection of the Siamese Government. Kĕlantan and Trĕnggânu still claim to be independent, though they send the *bûnga ămas*—or golden flower—to Bangkok once in three years. Pahang was placed under British Protection in 1888, and Johor is still independent, though its relations with the Government of Great Britain are very much the same as those which subsist between Siam and the Malay States of Kĕlantan and Trĕnggânu.

The *bûnga ămas*, to which reference has been made above, consists of two ornamental plants, with leaves and flowers, fashioned from gold and silver, and their value is estimated at about $5000. The sum necessary to defray the cost of these gifts is raised by means of a *banchi*, or poll-tax, to which every adult male contributes; and the return presents, sent from Bangkok, are of precisely the same value, and are, of course, a perquisite of the *Râja*. The exact significance of these gifts is a question of which very different views are taken by the parties concerned. The Siamese maintain that the *bûnga ămas* is a direct admission of suzerainty on the part of the *Râja* who sends it, while the Malay Sultâns and their Chiefs entirely deny this, and hold that it is merely *tanda s'pakat dan bĕr-sĕhâbat* —a token of alliance and friendship. It is not, perhaps, generally known that, as late as 1826, Pĕrak was in the habit of sending a similar gift to Siam, and that the British Government bound itself not to restrain the Sultân of Pêrak from continuing this practice if he had a mind to do so. From this it would seem that there is some grounds for the contention of Trĕnggânu and Kĕlantan that the *bûnga ămas* is a purely voluntary gift, sent as a token of friendship to a more powerful State, with which the sender desires to be on terms of amity. Be this how it may, it is certain that Sultân Mansûr of Trĕnggânu, who first sent the *bûnga ămas* to Siam in 1776, did so, not in compliance with any demand made by the Siamese Government, but because he deemed it wise to be on friendly terms with the only race in his vicinity which was capable, in his opinion, of doing him a hurt.

Direct interference in the Government of Kĕlantan and Trĕnggânu has been more than once attempted by the Siamese, during the last few years, strenuous efforts having been made to increase their influence on the East Coast of the Peninsula, since the visit of the King of Siam to the Malay States in 1890. In Trĕnggânu, all these endeavours have been of no avail, and the Siamese have abandoned several projects which were devised in order to give them a hold over this State. In Kĕlantan, internal troubles have aided Siamese intrigues, the present *Râja* and his late brother both having so insecure a seat upon their thrones that they readily made concessions to the Siamese in order to purchase their support. Thus, at the present time, the flag of the White Elephant floats at the mouth of the Kĕlantan river on State occasions, though the administration of the country is still entirely in the hands of the *Râja* and his Chiefs.

The methods of Malay rulers, when they are unchecked by extraneous influences, are very curious; and those who desire to see the Malay *Râja* and the Malay *raäyat* in their natural condition, must nowadays study life on the East Coast. Nowhere else has the Malay been so little changed by the advancing years, and those who are only acquainted with the West Coast and its people, as they are to-day, will find much to learn when they visit the Eastern sea-board.

Until British interference changed the conditions which existed in Pahang, that country was the best type of an independent Malay State in the Peninsula, and much that was to be seen and learned in Pahang, in the days before the appointment of a British Resident, cannot now be experienced in quite the same measure anywhere else. Both Trĕnggânu and Kĕlantan have produced their strong rulers—for instance, Băginda Ŭmar of Trĕnggânu, and the 'Red-mouthed Sultân' of Kĕlantan—but neither of the present *Râjas* can boast anything resembling the same personality and force of character, or are possessed of the same power and influence, as distinguished Sultân Âhmad Maätham Shah of Pahang, in the brave days before the coming of the white men.

In subsequent articles, I hope, by sketching a few events which have occurred in some of the States on the East Coast; by relating some characteristic incidents, many of which have come within my experience; and by descriptions of the conditions of life among the natives, as I have known them; to give my European readers some idea of a state of Society, wholly unlike anything to which they are accustomed, and which must inevitably be altered out of all recognition by the rapidly increasing influence of foreigners in the Malay Peninsula.

THE PEOPLE OF THE EAST COAST

> I have eaten your rice and salt.
> I have drunk the milk of your kine,
> The deaths ye died I have watched beside,
> And the lives that ye lived were mine.
> Is there aught that I did not share,
> In vigil, or toil, or ease,
> One joy or woe that I did not know,
> Dear hearts beyond the seas?
>
> KIPLING (adapted).

ALTHOUGH the States on the East Coast lie in very close proximity one with another, the people who inhabit them differ widely among themselves, not only in appearance, in costume, and in the dialects which they speak, but also in manners, customs, and character. The Pahang Malay, in his unregenerate state, thinks chiefly of deeds of arms, illicit love intrigues, and the sports which his religion holds to be sinful. He is a cock-fighter, a gambler, and a brawler; he has an overweening opinion of himself, his country, and his race; he is at once ignorant, irreligious, and unintellectual; and his arrogance has passed into a proverb.[1]

---

[1] Kêchek ânak Mălâka; bûal ânak Měnangkâbau; tîpu ânak Rămbau; bidaäh ânak Trěnggânu; pěn-âkut ânak Singapüra; pěn-jělok ânak Kělantan; sômbong ânak Pahang.
    Wheedlers are the men of Malacca; boasters the men of Měnang-

He has many good qualities also, and is, above all things, manly and reckless,—as those who know him well, and love him, can bear witness,—but his faults are very much on the surface, and he is at no pains to hide them, being proud rather than ashamed of the reputation which they cause him to bear. He is more gracefully built than are most other natives on the East Coast, he dresses within an inch of his life, and often carries the best part of his property on his back and about his person,—for, like all gamblers, he is hopelessly improvident. He is a sportsman as soon as he can walk upon his feet without the aid of the supporting *âdan*;[1] he is in love as a permanent arrangement, and will go to any length, and run any risk, in order to satisfy his desires; and, as he is exceedingly touchy, and quick to take offence, he frequently seems to be in the condition which is known as 'spoiling for a fight.' He is apt to 'buck' about the brave deeds of himself and his countrymen, in an untamed way which would discredit the Colonel of a Regiment—who is privileged to 'buck' because his officers cannot attempt to check him. He knows many strange tales of 'lamentable things done long ago and ill done'; he is extraordinarily loyal to his *Râjas* and Chiefs, who have not always acted in a way to inspire devotion; he is capable of the most disinterested affection; he loves his wives and his

---

kâbau; cheats the men of Rămbau; liars the men of Trĕnggânu; cowards the men of Singapore; thieves the men of Kĕlantan; and arrogant are the men of Pahang.

[1] Adan = A hand-rail by means of which Malay children are taught to stand and walk.

little ones dearly; and, if once he trusts a man, will do anything in the wide world at that man's bidding. He is clean in his habits; nice about his food and his surroundings; is generally cheery; and is blest with a saving sense of humour, provided that the joke is at the expense of neither himself nor his relations. Like many people who love field sports, he hates books almost as much as he hates work. He can never be induced to study his Scriptures, and he only prays under compulsion, and attends the mosque on Friday because he wishes to avoid a fine. He never works if he can help it, and often will not suffer himself to be induced or tempted into doing so by offers of the most extravagant wages. If, when promises and persuasion have failed, however, the magic word *krah* is whispered in his ears, he will come without a murmur, and work really hard for no pay, bringing with him his own supply of food. *Krah*, as everybody knows, is the system of forced labour which is a State perquisite in unprotected Malay countries, and an ancestral instinct, inherited from his fathers, seems to prompt him to comply cheerfully with this custom, when on no other terms whatsoever would he permit himself to do a stroke of work. When so engaged, he will labour as no other man will do. I have had Pahang Malays working continuously for sixty hours at a stretch, and all on a handful of boiled rice; but they will only do this for one they know, whom they regard as their Chief, and in whose sight they would be ashamed to murmur at the severity of the work, or to give in when all are sharing the strain in equal measure.

The natives of Trĕnggânu are of a very different type. First and foremost, they are men of peace. Their sole interest in life is the trade or occupation which they ply, and they have none of that pride of race and country, which is so marked in the Pahang Malay. All they ask is to be allowed to make money, to study, or to earn a livelihood unmolested; and they have none of that 'loyal passion' for their intemperate Kings, which is such a curious feature in the character of the people of Pahang, who have had to suffer many things at the hands of their *râjas*. When Băginda Ùmar conquered Trĕnggânu in 1837, the people submitted to him without a struggle, and, if a stronger than he had tried to wrest the country from him, the bulk of the people would most certainly have acquiesced once more with equal calmness.

Study, trade, the skill of the artisan, 'and fruitful strifes and rivalries of peace,' these are the things in which all the interests of the Trĕnggânu Malay are centred. From his earliest infancy he grows up in an atmosphere of books, and money and trade, and manufactures, and bargainings, and hagglings. He knows how to praise the goods he is selling, and how to depreciate the wares he is buying, almost as soon as he can speak; and the unblushing manner in which he will hold forth concerning the antiquity of some article which he has made with his own hands, and the entire absence of all *mauvaise honte* which he displays when detected in the fraud, have earned for him the reputation he proverbially bears of being the best liar in the Peninsula. The Pahang boy grows up amid talk of war and rumours of war, which makes him long to be a man that he may use his weapons, almost before he has learned to stand upon his feet. Not so the young idea of Trĕnggânu. Men go about armed, of course, for such is the custom in all Independent Malay States, but they have little skill with spear or knife, and, since a proficiency as a scholar, an artisan, or as a shrewd man of business wins more credit than does a reputation for valour, the people of Trĕnggânu generally grow up cowards, and are not very much ashamed of standing so confessed. In his own line, however, the Trĕnggânu Malay is far in advance of any other natives on the East Coast, or indeed in the Peninsula. He has generally read his *Kurân* through, from end to end, before he has reached his teens, and, as the Malay character differs but slightly from the Arabic, he thereafter often acquires a knowledge of how to read and write his own language.

But a study of the Muhammadan Scriptures is apt to breed religious animosity, in the crude oriental mind, and the race of local saints, who have succeeded one another at Pâloh for several generations, have been instrumental in fomenting this feeling. Ungku Saiyid of Pâloh—the 'local holy man' for the time being—like his prototype in the *Naulahka*, has done much to agitate the minds of the people, and to create a 'commotion of popular bigotry.' He is a man of an extraordinary personality. His features are those of the pure Arab caste, and they show the ultra-refinement of one who is pinched with long fasts and other ascetic practices. Moreover, he has the unbounded vanity and self-conceit which is born of long years of adulation, and is infected by that touch of madness which breeds 'Cranks' in modern Europe, and 'Saints' in modern Asia. He preaches to crowded congregations thrice weekly, and the men of Trĕnggânu flock from all parts of the country to sit at his feet. The Sultân, too, like his father, and his great-uncle, Băginda Ŭmar, has been at some pains to ensure the performance of religious rites by all his people, and, as far as outward observances go, he appears to have been successful. Moreover, the natives of Trĕnggânu love religious and learned discussions of all kinds, and most of them:

> When young, do eagerly frequent
> Doctor and Saint and hear great argument
> About it and about,

though, like poor Omar, they never seem to arrive at any conclusions which have not previously been used by them as a starting-point. All this makes for fanaticism,—which, however, with so cowardly a people, is more likely to be noisy than violent,—and all such sinful sports as cock-fighting, bull fights, gambling, and the like, are forbidden by law to the people of Trĕnggânu. In spite of all this, however, the natives of this State do not really lead lives in any degree more clean than is customary among other Malays. Their morals are, for the most part, those of the streets of London after eleven o'clock on a Saturday night.

It is as an artisan, however, that the Trĕnggânu Malay really excels. The best products of their looms, the brass and nickel utensils, some of the weapons, and most of the woodwork fashioned in Trĕnggânu, are the best native made wares, of their kind, in the Peninsula, and the extreme ingenuity with which they imitate the products of other States, or Islands of the Archipelago, is quite unrivalled in this part of the world. Silk *sárongs*, in close imitation of those woven in Pahang and Kĕlantan, are made cheap, and sold as the genuine articles. Bales of the white turban cloths, flecked with gold thread, which are so much worn by men who have returned from the *Haj*, are annually exported to Mecca, where they are sold, as articles of real Arabic manufacture, to the confiding pilgrims. All these silks and cloths fade and wear out with inconceivable rapidity, but, until this occurs, the purchaser is but rarely able to detect the fraud of which he has been a victim. Weapons, too, are made in exact imitation of those produced by the natives of Celebes or Java, and it is often not until the silver watering on the blades begins to crack and peel—like paint on a plank near a furnace—that their real origin becomes known. At the present time, the artisans of Trĕnggânu are largely engaged in making exact imitations of the local currency, to the exceeding dolor of the Sultân, and with no small profit to themselves.

In appearance, the Trĕnggânu Malay is somewhat larger boned, broader featured, and more clumsily put together than is the typical Pahang Malay. He also dresses somewhat differently, and it is easy to detect the nationality of a Trĕnggânu man, even before he opens his mouth in speech. The difference in appearance is subtle, and to one who is not used to Malays, the natives of Pahang, Kĕlantan, and Trĕnggânu have nothing to distinguish them one from another, whereas, after a year or two on the East Coast, what at first are almost imperceptible differences, are soon recognised as being widely distinguishing marks.

The Kĕlantan man is, to the native of Pahang, what the water-buffalo is to a short-horn. To begin with, to the uninitiated he is wholly unintelligible. He grunts at one like the fatted pig at the Agricultural Shows, and expects one to understand the meaning which he attaches to these grunts. This proves him to be sanguine but unintelligent. He cannot understand any dialect but his own,—which is convincing evidence to non-Kĕlantan Malays that he is a born fool,—and he is apt to complain bitterly of the accents of strangers, whereas, to all but his own countrymen, it is *his* accent which appears to be the real grievance. He is plain of face, fat, ugly, and ungainly of body, huge as to the hands and feet, not scrupulously clean in his person and habits, and, like most very fleshy people, he is blessed with an exceedingly even temper, and is excessively happy, good-natured, and stolid. He can break open a door by butting it with his head, and the door is the only sufferer. [Âwang Kĕpâla Kras—Âwang of the Hard Head—who is a Kĕlantan Malay, backs himself to butt a trained fighting ram out of time!] He can lift great weights, walk long distances, pole or paddle a boat for many hours at a stretch, and can, and does, work more than any other Malay.

This huge mass of fleshy brown humanity is reared on a pound or two of boiled rice, and a few shreds of fish. To see him eat is to be attacked with a lasting loathing for food. He takes in his rice as though stoking a steamboat. The coal shovel is his ponderous fist, and the extent to which his cheeks are capable of stretching alone regulates the size of his mouthfuls. He is, in every way, coarser-grained than any other Malay. He has much less self-respect; is rarely touchy and sensitive, as are other natives of the Peninsula; and when he is brave, it is with the courage of the blind, who know not the extent of the danger which they are facing. An utter want of imagination goes to the making of more heroes than it is pleasant to think about, since people who cannot picture consequences, and forecast risks, deserve but little credit for the courage which they display, but are unable to appreciate.

To his neighbours on the East Coast, however, all the other remarkable characteristics of the Kĕlantan Malay are lost sight of, or rather, are completely overshadowed, by his reputation as a thief among thieves. In vain have successive generations of Kĕlantan *râjas* cut off the hands, feet, and heads of detected or suspected burglars and robbers; in vain have all sorts of stratagems been adopted by travellers as precautions against thieves; and in vain have the families of convicted men been punished for the deeds of their relations. Nothing, apparently, can stamp out the instinct which prompts high and low, rich and poor, to take possession of any property belonging to someone else whenever the opportunity offers. Men with flocks and herds, and *pâdi* swamps, and fruit orchards, steal if they get the chance just as much as does the indigent peasant who has sold his last child into slavery for three dollars in cash. Most of the great chiefs of the country do not steal in person, but they keep bands of paid ruffians who do that work for them, in return for their protection, and a share of the takings. The skill with which some Kĕlantan Malays pick a pocket, and the ingenuity displayed in their burglaries, would not discredit a pupil of Fagin the Jew; and robbery with violence is almost equally common. Their favourite weapon is an uncanny looking instrument called *pârang jĕngok* — or the 'peeping' knife—which is armed with a sharp peak at the tip, standing out almost at right angles to the rest of the blade. Armed with this, on a dark night, the robber walks down a street, and just as he passes a man, he strikes back over his left shoulder, so that the peak catches his victim in the back of the head, and knocks him endways. He can then be robbed with ease and comfort, and, whether he recovers from the blow or dies from its effects is his own affair, and concerns the thief not at all. It is not very long ago since two men were found lying senseless in the streets of Kôta Bharu, each having put the other *hors de combat* with a *pârang jĕngok*, striking at the same moment, in the same way, and with the same amiable intention. To save further trouble they each had their hands cut off, as soon as they came round, by the Sultân's order. This, when you come to think of it, was a sound course for the Sultân to pursue.

The women of Kĕlantan are, many of them, well favoured enough. They are, for the most part, fine upstanding wenches, somewhat more largely built than most Malay women, and they appear more in public than is usual in the Peninsula. At Kôta Bharu, women, both young and old, crowd the markets at all hours of the day, and do most of the selling and buying. They converse freely with strangers, go about unveiled, and shew no signs of that affected bashfulness, which cloaks the very indifferent morals of the average Malay woman, but which it is a point of honour with her to assume when in the presence of men.

In Këlantan, both men and women dress differently from Malays in other States. The men wear neither coats nor trousers, but they bind a *sârong* and three or four sashes about their waists. The *sârong* generally comes down to the knee, and, when seated, the knee-caps are often exposed, even in the King's *Bâlai*,—a practice that would not be tolerated in any other part of the Peninsula. The women also dispense with an upper garment, and make up the deficiency by a lavish use of *sârong* and scarves. The shoulders and upper portion of the chest, however, are left bare. These and other practices, cause the Këlantan Malays to be much despised by the peoples of other Native States, who regard them as unmannerly and uncouth. Indeed, prior to 1888, few Këlantan men dared to set foot in Pahang, for, as an old Chief once said in my presence, the only use a Pahang native had for a Këlantan Malay, before the coming of the white men, was 'as a thing wherewith to sharpen the blade of his dagger,' and this, be it remembered, is not a mere *façon de parler*.

After straining my jaws, doing violence to my tongue, and racking my throat, I have acquired a working knowledge of the Kĕlantan *patois*, and can now understand and speak it almost as easily as I do the more refined dialects. This has helped me to, in some degree, understand the people, and, though they have many bad qualities, I like them. In a rude, rough way, and without the swagger of the Pahang Malay, they are sportsmen. I shot over one of them for four years, and, until he went blind, he was as good a retriever as one would desire to possess. At Kôta Bharu bull fights, matches between rams, cocks, quails, and human prize fighters, are the chief amusement of the people. The latter sport is peculiar to Kĕlantan. The fights begin with the ungainly posturing, and aimless gesticulation, with which all who have witnessed a Malay sword-dance are familiar, but when the fencers come to close quarters the interest begins. They strike, kick, pinch, bite, scratch, and even spit, until one or the other is unable to move. No time is called, catch as catch can, and strike as best, and where best you may, are the simple rules of these contests, and the sight is a somewhat degrading and unpleasant one, though it excites the spectators to ecstasies of delight and laughter. Most big Chiefs in Kĕlantan keep trained men to take part in these prize fights, and heavy bets are made on the result.

And the life of these people? Whether in Pahang, Trĕnggânu, or Kĕlantan it is much the same. Up country the natives live more chastely than do the people of the capital; they work harder, age sooner, lie less softly, experience less change, and are chiefly occupied in supporting themselves and their families. They rise early, work or idle through the day, and go to bed very soon after dark. Their lives are entirely monotonous, dull, and uneventful, but the knowledge of other and better things is not for them, and they live contentedly the only life of which they have any experience. They can rarely afford to support more than one wife, and, as they love their little ones dearly, they often live with the same woman all the days of her life, since divorce entails some degree of separation from the children.

Down country things are different. The gossip of the Court, the tales of brave deeds, the learned discussions, or the rough sports add an interest to life, which is not to be experienced by the dwellers in the far interior. The number of unmarried women within the palace causes the youths of the town to plunge wildly into intrigues, for which they often have to pay a heavy price, but which always instil an element of romance into their lives. This, of course, is the merest sketch, for no real study of the people can be attempted in a work written on such unscientific lines as the present, and the reader—supposing such a problematical person to exist—must form his own picture of my Malay friends from the stories which I shall have to tell in future pages. It is only too probable that I shall fail to give any real idea of the people of whom I write, to any save those who are already able to fill in the omissions for themselves, and who, therefore, know as much about Malays as is good for any man; but, if I fail, it will be because I lack the skill to depict with vividness the lives of those whom I know intimately, and whom, in spite of all their faults, and foibles, and ignorance, and queer ways, I love exceedingly.

THE EXPERIENCES OF RÂJA HAJI HAMID

> I've spent my life in war and strife,
>   And now I'm waxing old ;
> I've planned and wrought, and dared and fought,
>   And all my tale is told ;
> I've made my kill, and felt the chill
>   Of blades that stab and hew,
> And my only theme, as I sit and dream,
>   Is the deeds I was wont to do.

These things were told me by Râja Haji Hamid, as he and I lay smoking on our mats during the cool, still hours before the dawn. He was a Sĕlângor man who had accompanied me to the East Coast, as chief of my followers, a band of ruffians, who at that time were engaged in helping me to act as 'the bait at the tip of the fish-hook,' in an Independent Malay State— to use the phrase then current among my people.

We had passed the evening in the King's *Bâlai* watching the Chinamen raking in their gains, whi l the Malays gambled and cursed their luck, with much slapping of thighs, and frequent references to God and his Prophet,—according to whose teaching gaming is an unclean thing. The sight of the play, and of the fierce passions which it aroused, had awakened memories in Râja Haji's mind, and it was evidently not without a pang that he remembered that the turban round his head,—which his increasing years, and his manifold sins, had driven him to Mecca to seek,—forbade him to partake publicly in the unholy sport. Like most of those who have outgrown their pleasant vices, he had a hearty admiration for his old, prodigal, unregenerate self; and, as I lay listening, he spoke lovingly of the old days at Sĕlângor, before the coming of the white men.

'Allah Tûan! I loved those old times exceedingly! When the Company had not yet come to Sĕlângor, when all were shy of Si-Hamid, and none dared face his *kris*, the "Chinese Axe." I never felt the grip of poverty in those times, for my supplies were ever at the tip of my dagger, and they were few who dared withhold aught which I desired or coveted!'

'Did I ever tell thee, *Tûan*, the tale of how the gamblers of Klang yielded up the money of their banks to me without resistance; or the turn of a dice box? No? Ah, that was a pleasant tale, and a deed which was famous throughout Sĕlângor, and gave me a very great name.

'It was in this wise. I was in a sorry case, for the boats had ceased to ply on the river through fear of me, and my followers were few, so that I could not rush a town or a Chinese *kongsi* house. As for the village people, they were as poor as I, and, save for their women-folk, I never harassed them. Now, one day, my wives and people came to me asking for rice, or for money wherewith to purchase it, and I had nothing to give them, only one little dollar remaining to me.

It is very bad when the little ones want food, and my liver grew hot at the thought. None of the woman-folk dared to say any word, when they saw that my eyes waxed red; but the little children cried, and I heard them, and was sad. Moreover, I, too, was hungry, for my belly was empty. Then I looked upon my only dollar, and, calling one of my men, I bade him go to a Chinese store, and buy me a bottle of the white man's perfume. Now, when one of my wives, the mother of my son, heard this order she cried out in anger: "Art thou mad, Father of Che' Bûjang? Art thou mad, that thou throwest away thy last dollar on perfumes for thy lights of love, while Che' Bûjang and his brethren cry for rice?" But I slapped her on the mouth, and said "Be still!"—for it is not well for a man to suffer a woman to question the doings of men.

'That evening, when the night had fallen, I put on my fighting-jacket, and my Celebes drawers, and bound my *kris*, the "Chinese Axe," about my waist, and took my sword, the "Rising Sun," in my hand. Three or four of my boys followed at my back, and I did not forget to take with me the bottle of the white man's perfume. I made straight for the great Klang gambling house, and when I reached the door, I halted for the space of an eye-flick, and spilled the scent over my hand and arm as far as the elbow. Then I rushed in among the gamblers, suddenly and without warning, stepping like a fencer in the sword-dance and crying "*Amok! Amok!*" till the coins danced upon the gaming tables. All the gamblers stayed their hands from the staking, and some seized their dagger hilts. Then

I cried aloud three times, "I am Si-Hamid, the Tiger Unbound!"—for by that name did men then call me—"Get ye to your dwellings speedily, and leave your money where it is, or I will slay you!"

'Many were affrighted, some laughed, some hesitated, but none did as I bade them. "Dogs and pigs!" I cried, "Are your ears deaf that ye obey me not, or are ye sated with life, and desire that your shrouds should be prepared? Obey me, or I will slay ye all, as a kite swoops upon little chickens! What is your power, and what are your stratagems, and how can ye prevail against me? I who am invulnerable, I whom even the fire burns but cannot devour!"

'With that I thrust my right hand into the flame of a gaming lamp, and it, being saturated with the white man's perfume, blazed up bravely even to my elbow, doing me no hurt, as I waved my arm above my head. Verily, the white men are very clever, who so cunningly devise the medicine of these perfumes.

'Now, when all the people in the gambling house saw that my arm and hand burned with fire, but were not consumed, a great fear fell upon them, and they fled shrieking, and no man stayed to gather up his silver. This I presently put into sacks, and my men removed it to my house, and my fame waxed very great in Klang. Men said that henceforth Si-Hamid should be named the Fiery Rhinoceros,[1] and not the Unbound Tiger, as they had hitherto called me. It was long ere the trick became known, and even then no man, among those who were within the

[1] Fiery Rhinoceros = Bâdak âpi, a fabulous monster of Malay tradition.

gaming house that night, dared ask me for the money which I had borrowed from him and his fellows. Ya Allah, Tûan, but those days were exceeding good days! I cannot think upon them, for it makes me sad. It is true what is said in the *pantun* of the men of Kĕdah:

> ' Pûlau Pînang has a new town,
> And Captain Light is its King ;
> Do not recall the days that are gone,
> Or you will bow down your head,
> And the tears will gush forth !

'Ya Allah! Ya Tûhan-ku! Verily, I cannot think upon it!'

He tossed about uneasily on his mat for some time, and I let him be, for the memory of the old, free days to a Malay *râja*, whose claws have been cut by the Europeans, is like new wine when it comes back suddenly upon him, and it is best, I think, to let a man fight out such troubles alone and in silence. 'Can words make foul things fair?'—and, however much I might sympathise with my friend, there was no blinking the fact, that he and I were then engaged in trying to do for another set of Malay *râjas*, all that Raja Haji Hamid so bitterly regretted that the white men had done for him, and for Sĕlângor.

After a space he became calmer, for though the thought of his troubles is often present to the mind of a Malay *râja*, the paroxysms, which the memory occasions, are not usually of long duration. Presently he began chuckling to himself, and then spoke again :

'I remember once, when I was for the moment rich with the spoils of war, I gambled all the evening in that same house at Klang, and lost four thousand dollars. It mattered not at all on which quarter of the mat I staked, nor whether I staked *ko-o*, *li-am*, or *tang*; I pursued the red half of the dice as one chases a dog, but never once did I catch it. At last, when my four thousand dollars were finished, I arose and departed, and my liver was hot in my chest. As I came out of the Farm, a Chinaman, whom I knew, and who loved me, followed after me, and said, "Hai-yah, Ungku, you have lost much to-night. That man with whom you gambled was cheating you, for he has a trick whereby he can make the red part of the dice turn to whichever side of the mat he wills." "Is this true?" I asked, and he said, "It is indeed true."'

'Then I loosened the "Chinese Axe" in its scabbard, and turned back into the Farm. First I seized the Chinaman by the pig-tail, and my followers gathered up all the money in the bank, near seven thousand dollars, so that it needed six men to carry it, and I then departed to my house, none daring to bar my passage.'

'When we had entered the house, I bade the Chinaman be seated, and told him that I would kill him, even then, if he did not show me the trick whereby he had cheated me. This he presently did, and for near two hours I sat watching him, and practising, for I had a mind to learn the manner of his art, thinking that hereafter I might profit by it. Then, when the dawn was breaking, I led the Chinaman down to the river by the hand,—for I was loth to make a mess within my house,—and when I had cut his throat, and sent his body floating down-stream, I washed myself, performed my ablutions before prayer, prayed, and went to my bed, for my eyes were heavy with sleep.'

'*Kasih-an China!*' I said, 'I am sorry for the Chinaman!'

'Why are you sorry for him?' asked Raja Haji, 'He had cheated me and it was not fitting that he should live; besides, he was a Chinaman, and we counted not their lives as being of any worth. In Kinta, before Mr. Birch went to Pêrak, they had a game called *Main China*, each man betting on the number of the coins which a passing Chinaman carried in his pouch, and whether they were odd or even. Thereafter, when the bets had been made, they would kill the Chinaman and count the coins.'

'They might have done that without killing the Chinaman,' I said.

'It is true,' rejoined Râja Haji, 'but it was a more certain way, and, moreover, it increased their pleasure. But *Tûan*, the night is very far advanced. Let us sleep.'

Verily, life in an Independent Malay State, like adversity, makes one acquainted with strange bedfellows.

THE BATTLE OF THE WOMEN

Woman is the lesser man, and all her passions matched with mine,
Are as moonlight unto sunlight, and as water unto wine.
Locksley Hall.

THIS is a true story. Also, unlike most of the tales which I have to tell concerning my Malay friends, it is garnished with a moral; and one, moreover, which the Women's Rights Committees would do well to note. I should dearly like to print it as a tract, for distribution to these excellent and loud-talking institutions, but, failing that, I publish it here, among its unworthy companions.

To those who live in and around a Malay Court, two things only take rank as the serious matters of life. These are the love intrigues, in which all are more or less engaged at peril of their lives, and the deeds of daring and violence,—long past or newly done,—of discussing which men and women alike never weary. People talk, think, and dream of little else, not only in the places where men congregate, but also in the dimly lit inner apartments, where the women are gathered together. In the conduct of their love intrigues, men and women alike take a very active part, for the ladies of the Peninsula are as often as not the wooers of the men, and a Malay girl does not hesitate to make the necessary advances if the swain is slow to take the initiative, or fails to perceive the desire which she has conceived for him. In the matter of fighting, however, the women—who are as often as not the cause—act usually as mere spectators, taking no active part themselves, though they join in a shrill chorus of applause when a shrewd blow is given, and delight greatly in the brave doings of their men. Nevertheless, the warlike atmosphere, with which she is surrounded all the days of her life, sometimes infects a young Malay Princess, and urges her to do some daring deed which shall emulate the exploits of her brothers, and shall show her admirers how dashing a spirit, and how great a courage are hers.

It was during the hot, aching months, which, in Merry England, go to make up the Spring of the year; and the King and his favourite concubines had betaken themselves up-river to snare turtle-doves, and to drowse away the hours in the cool flowering fruit groves, and under the shade of the lilac-coloured *bûngor* trees. Therefore the youths and maidens in the palace were having a good time, and were gaily engaged in sowing the whirlwind, with a sublime disregard for the storm, which it would be theirs to reap, when the King returned to punish. As the vernacular proverb has it, the cat and the roast, the tinder and the spark, and a boy and a girl are ill to keep asunder; and consequently my friends about the palace were often in trouble, by reason of their love affairs, even when the King was at hand; and on his return, after he had been absent for a day or two, there was generally the very devil to pay. Perhaps, on this occasion, the extreme heat had something to do with it, and made hot blood surge through young veins with unwonted fury, for things went even worse than usual, and, after a week of flagrant and extraordinary ill-doing, Tŭngku Indut, one of the King's sons, put the finishing touch to it all, by eloping with no less than four of his father's choicest dancing girls!

Now, these girls were as the apple of her eye to Tŭngku Indut's half-sister, Tŭngku Amînah. They belonged to her mother's household, and had been trained to dance from earliest infancy, with infinite care and pains. Nor had they attained their present degree of efficiency, without the twisting back of tortured fingers, and sundry other gentle punishments, dear to Malay ladies, being frequently resorted to, in order to quicken their intelligence. That her brother should now carry off these girls, after all the trouble which had been expended upon their education, was a sore offence to Tŭngku Amînah; and that the girls themselves were very willing captives, and had found a princely lover, while she remained unwedded, did not tend to soothe her gentle woman's breast. Her mother was also very wroth, and sent threatening messages to Tŭngku Indut, presaging blood and thunder, and other grievous trouble when the King returned. Tŭngku Indut, however, resolutely declined to give the girls up. He knew that he had gone so far that no tardy amends could now cover his ill-deeds, and, as he had a fancy for the girls, he decided to enjoy the goods the gods had sent him until his father came back, and the day of reckoning arrived. His stepmother, therefore, resigned herself to await the King's return; but Tŭngku Amînah could not brook delay, and she resolved to attack Tŭngku Indut in his house, and to wrest the girls from him by force of arms.

Circumstances favoured her, as her mother, who was the only person capable of thwarting her project, was ill with fever, and had retired early to her bed and her opium pipe. Tŭngku Amînah was thus left at liberty to do whatsoever she wished; and accordingly, at about eleven o'clock that night, she sallied forth, from within the stone wall which surrounded her mother's palace, at the head of her army.

It was at this moment that word was brought to me that strange things were toward, and I, and the Malays who were with me, ran out to our compound fence, and witnessed all that ensued with our eyes glued to the chinks in the plaited bamboos.

Presently the army came pouring down the street in the pale moonlight, and halted in front of my compound, which chanced to face the house at that time occupied by Tŭngku Indut, the door of which abutted on the main thoroughfare. Tŭngku Amînah led the van, strutting along with an arrogant and truculent swagger most laughable to see. She was dressed for the occasion after the fashion of the Malay warrior. Her body was encased in a short-sleeved, tight-fitting fighting jacket, which only served to emphasise the femininity of her bust. She wore striped silk breeches reaching to the middle of her shins; a silk *sârong* was folded short about her waist; and her thick hair was tucked away beneath a head handkerchief twisted into a peak in the manner called *tanjak*. At her belt she carried a *kris*, and also, a smaller dagger, called a 'pepper-crusher' in the vernacular, and in her hand she held a drawn sword, which she brandished as she walked. At her back came some three hundred women, moving down the street with that queer half-tripping, half-running gait, which Malay women always affect when they go abroad in a crowd at the heel of their Princess. The way in which they run into and press against one another, on such occasions, together with the little quick short steps they take, always reminds me of young chickens trying to seek shelter under their mother's wing. The army was wonderfully and fearfully armed. Some of the more fortunate had spears and daggers; one or two carried old swords; but the majority were armed with weapons borrowed from the cook-house. The axes and choppers, used for breaking up firewood, were the best of these arms, but the number of these was limited, most of Tŭngku Amînah's gallant three hundred being provided with no better weapons than the *kandar* sticks, on which water pails are carried; spits made of wood hardened in the fire; cocoa-nut scrapers lashed to sticks; and a few old pocket-knives and fish-spears. What they lacked in equipment, however, they made up in noise, one and all combining to raise an indescribable and deafening babel.

As they halted before Tŭngku Indut's house, the shrill screams of defiance from three hundred dainty throats pierced my ear-drums like a steam siren, and they were all so marvellously noisy, brave, and defiant, that, in spite of an occasional girlish giggle from one or another of them, I began to fear there would be bad trouble before the dawn. So wild was their excitement, and so maddening was the din they made, that, though Tŭngku Amînah shrieked louder than any one of them, she could not make herself heard above the tumult; and it was not until she had scratched the faces of those nearest to her, and smitten others with the flat of her sword, that she succeeded in reducing her followers to even a partial silence. Then she beat upon the barred door of Tŭngku Indut's house with her naked weapon, and cried shrilly to her brother:—

'Come forth, Indut! Come forth, if thou art in truth the son of the same father as myself! Come forth!'

'Come forth!' echoed the army, and the deafening din of defiance broke out once more, and was again with difficulty repressed by Tŭngku Amînah.

'Come forth!' she shrilled once more, 'come forth that I may rip thy belly, and cause thy entrails to gush out upon the ground!'

'Come forth, thou accursed and ill-omened one!' echoed the army, with the unanimity of Pickwick's thirty boarders.

Indut, however, did not show any signs of coming forth; but when the women had screamed themselves hoarse and out of breath, his gruff voice sounded from within the house, like the growl of a wild beast, after all that shrill feminine yelping.

'Go hence, Iang!' he shouted, 'get thee to thy bed, thou foolish one; disturb not one who desires to slumber, and waken not the fowls with thy unmaidenly shouting.'

Now, when Tŭngku Amînah heard these words she dropped her sword, and beat upon the door with her little bare hands, weeping and screaming in a perfect ecstasy of rage, and showering curses and imprecations on her brother. The army joined in the torrent of abuse, and a very pretty set of phrases were sent spinning through the clean night air. At length, Tŭngku Amînah, finding that she only bruised her hands, again took up her sword, and, as soon as she could make herself heard, renewed her challenge to her brother to come forth.

When this scene had continued for about twenty minutes, and I was beginning to fear that the Devil would prompt Tŭngku Amînah to fire her brother's house, and that I should get burned out also,—suffering, as the Malays says, like the woodpecker in the falling tree,—a sudden and unexpected turn was given to affairs, which speedily brought things to an abrupt conclusion.

During one of the pauses for breath, indulged in by the clamouring women, Tŭngku Indut was heard to arise from his couch with great noise and deliberation. A hushed silence immediately fell upon the assembled women, and, in the stillness, Tŭngku Indut's words were distinctly heard by all of us.

'Âwang!' he said, naming one of his followers, 'Âwang! *Bring me my sword!*'

That was all, but it was enough and to spare. A shrill shriek was raised by the listening women,—a shriek, this time, of fear and not of defiance,—and in a moment the army of three hundred ladies was in full flight. Never was there such a rout. They tumbled over, and trampled upon one another in their frantic desire to escape, and maimed one another, as they fought their way up the narrow roadway, in their panic. All respect for persons, rank, or position, was completely lost sight of, commoners pushing past *rájas* in their deadly fear of being the hindermost, who is the proverbial prey of the pursuing devil. Too breathless to scream, and sweating with fear and exertion, they scuffled up the street, to the sound of rending garments and pattering feet, nor did they rest until the palace was regained, and the doors securely barred.

On the King's return, the dancing girls were, of course, surrendered; and I do not like to think what was the measure of bodily pain and suffering, that these dainty creatures were called upon to pay as the price of their escapade. It was a sore subject with Tŭngku Indut, too, and he and his father were not on speaking terms, on this account, for near a twelvemonth after.

As for Tŭngku Amînah, she is as truculent as ever, and bears a great reputation for courage among her fellow country-women. It is not every girl, they say, who would so boldly have attacked; and of the retreat, which only a few of us witnessed, no mention is ever made.

One has heard of the Women's Rights Meeting in Boston, which was broken up in confusion by the untimely appearance of three little mice; and of that other meeting, in which the aid of the Chairwoman's husband and brothers had to be sought, in order to eject a solitary derisive man, who successfully defied the assembled emancipated females to move him from his position; but neither of these stories seems to me to illustrate the inherent feebleness of women, when unaided by the ruder sex, quite as forcibly as does the pleasant story of Tŭngku Amînah and her brother, Tŭngku Indut.

IN COCK-PIT AND BULL-RING

> There's joy in all sport, no matter the sort,
>   In each game that is fought for and won;
> There's joy in the skill, that helps to a kill,
>   Be the weapon, rod, spear, or gun.
> There's joy in the chase, in the rush of a race,
>   In all that is fierce and strong;
> There's joy in the strife, that is war to the knife,
>   Let those who will, brand it as wrong.
> But no joy that we know, in our life here below,
>   For man, or for bird, or for cattle,
> Can come within sight of the gorgeous delight,
>   The glorious frenzy of battle!

TAKING them by and large the Malays have no bowels. Physical pain, even if endured by human beings, excites in them but little sympathy or compassion, and to the beasts that perish they are often almost as wantonly cruel as an English drayman. The theory that men owe any duties to the lower animals, is one which the Malays cannot be readily made to understand; and the idea of cruelty to a beast can only be expressed in their language by a long and roundabout sentence. The Malays can hardly be blamed for this perhaps, seeing that, even among our immaculate selves, a consideration for animals is of comparatively modern origin, and the people of the Peninsula, as I have been at some pains to show, are in their ideas on many subjects, much what our ancestors were some hundreds of years ago. A few animals, however, are hedged about and protected by some ancient superstition, the origin of which is now totally forgotten, but even these do not escape scot free. Thus, it is a common belief among Malays, that, if a cat is killed, he who takes its life, will in the next world, be called upon to carry and pile logs of wood, as big as cocoa-nut trees, to the number of the hairs on the beast's body. Therefore cats are not *killed;* but, if they become too daring in their raids on the hen-coop, or the food rack, they are tied to a raft and sent floating down-stream, to perish miserably of hunger. The people of the villages, by which they pass, make haste to push the raft out again into mid-stream, should it in its passage adhere to bank or bathing hut, and on no account is the animal suffered to land. To any one who thinks about it, this long and lingering death is infinitely more cruel than one caused by a blow from an axe, but the Malays do not trouble to consider such a detail, and would care little if they did.

In spite of the stupid callousness with regard to pain inflicted on animals, of which this is an instance, the Malays are not as a race cruel in the sports wherein animals take a part, and, on the East Coast especially, little objection can be raised, save by the most strait-laced and sentimental, to the manner in which both cock and bull-fights are conducted. Many, of course, hold that it is morally wrong to cause any animals to do battle one with another, and this is also the teaching of the Muhammadan religion. The Malays, however, have not yet learned to breathe the rarefied atmosphere, which can only be inhaled in comfort, by the frequenters of Exeter Hall, and, seeing that Allah has implanted an instinct of combat in many animals, the Malays take no shame in deriving amusement from the fact.

In the Archipelago, and on the West Coast of the Peninsula, cock-fights are conducted in the manner known to the Malays as *bĕr-tâji*, the birds being armed with long artificial spurs, sharp as razors, and curved like a Malay woman's eyebrow. These weapons make cruel wounds, and cause the death of one or another of the combatants, almost before the sport has well begun. To the Malay of the East Coast, this form of cock-fighting is regarded as stupid and unsportsmanlike, an opinion which I fully share. It is the marvellous pluck and endurance of the birds, that lend an interest to a cock-fight,—qualities which are in no way required, if the birds are armed with weapons, other than those with which they are furnished by nature.

A cock-fight between two well-known birds is a serious affair in Pahang. The rival qualities of the combatants have furnished food for endless discussion for weeks, or even months before, and every one of standing has visited and examined the cocks, and has made a book upon the event. On the day fixed for the fight, a crowd collects before the palace, and some of the King's youths set up the cock-pit, which is a ring, about three feet in diameter, enclosed by canvas walls, supported on stakes driven into the ground.

Presently the *Juâra*, or cock-fighters, appear, each carrying his bird under his left arm. They enter the cock-pit, squat down, and begin pulling at, and shampooing the legs and wings of their birds, in the manner which Malays believe loosen the muscles, and get the reefs out of the cocks' limbs. Then the word is given to start the fight, and the birds, released, fly straight at one another, striking with their spurs, and sending feathers flying in all directions. This lasts for perhaps three minutes, when the cocks begin to lose their wind, and the fight is carried on as much with their beaks as with their spurs. Each bird tries to get its head under its opponent's wing, running forward to strike at the back of its antagonist's head, as soon as its own emerges from under its temporary shelter. This is varied by an occasional blow with the spurs, and the Malays herald each stroke with loud cries of approval. *Bâsah! Bâsah!* Thou hast wetted him! Thou has drawn blood! *Ah itu dia!* That is it! That is a good one! *Ah sâkit-lah itu!* Ah, that was a nasty one! And the birds are exhorted to make fresh efforts, amid occasional bursts of the shrill chorus of yells, called *sôrak*, their backers cheering them on, and crying to them by name.

Presently time is called, the watch being a small section of cocoa-nut in which a hole has been bored, that is set floating on the surface of a jar of water, until it gradually becomes filled and sinks. At the word, each cock-fighter seizes his bird, drenches it with water, cleans out with a feather the phlegm which has collected in its throat, and shampoos its legs and body. Then, at the given word, the birds are again released, and they fly at one another with renewed energy. They loose their wind more speedily this time, and thereafter they pursue the tactics already described, until time is again called. When some ten rounds have been fought, and both the birds are beginning to show signs of distress, the interest of the contest reaches its height, for the fight is at an end if either bird raises its back feathers, in a peculiar manner, by which cocks declare themselves to be vanquished. Early in the tenth round the right eye-ball of one cock is broken, and, shortly after, the left eye is bunged up, so that for the time it is blind. Nevertheless, it refuses to throw up the sponge, and fights on gallantly to the end of the round, taking terrible punishment, and doing but little harm to its opponent. One cannot but be full of pity and admiration for the brave bird, which thus gives so marvellous an example of its pluck and endurance. At last time is called, and the cockfighter, who is in charge of the blinded bird, after examining it carefully, asks for a needle and thread, and the swollen lower lid of the still uninjured eye-ball is sewn to the piece of membrane on the bird's cheek, and its sight is thus once more partially restored. Again time is called, and the birds resume their contest, the cock with the injured eye repaying its adversary so handsomely for the punishment which it had received in the previous round, that, before the cocoa-nut shell is half full of water, its opponent has surrendered, and has immediately been snatched up by the keeper in charge of it. The victorious bird, draggled and woebegone, with great patches of red flesh showing through its wet plumage, with the membrane of its face, and its short gills and comb swollen and bloody, with one eye put out, and the other only kept open by the thread attached to its eyelid, yet makes shift to strut, with staggering gait, across the cock-pit, and to notify its victory, by giving vent to a lamentable ghost of a crow. Then it is carried off followed by an admiring, gesticulating, vociferous crowd, to be elaborately tended and nursed, as befits so gallant a bird. The beauty of the sport is that either bird can stop fighting at any moment. They are never forced to continue the conflict if once they have declared themselves defeated, and the only real element of cruelty is thus removed. The birds in fighting, follow the instinct which nature has implanted in them, and their marvellous courage and endurance surpass anything to be found in any other animals, human or otherwise, with which I am acquainted. Most birds fight more or less; from the little fierce quail, to the sucking doves which ignorant Europeans, before their illusions have been dispelled by a sojourn in the East, are accustomed to regard as the emblems of peace and purity; but no bird, or beast, or fish, or human being fights so well, or takes such pleasure in the fierce joy of battle, as does a plucky, lanky, ugly, hard-bit old fighting-cock.

The Malays regard these birds with immense respect, and value their fighting-cocks next to their children. A few years ago, a boy, who was in charge of a cock which belonged to a *Râja* of my acquaintance, accidentally pulled some feathers from the bird's tail. 'What did you do that for? Devil!' cried the *Râja*.

'It was not done on purpose Ungku!' said the boy.

'Thou art marvellous clever at repartee!' quoth the Prince, and, so saying, he lifted a billet of wood, which chanced to be lying near at hand, and smote the boy on the head so that he died.

'That will teach my people to have a care how they use my fighting-cocks!' said the *Râja;* and that was his servant's epitaph.

'It is a mere boyish prank,' said the father of the young *Râja,* when the matter was reported to him, 'and moreover it is well that he should slay one or two with his own hand, else how should men learn to fear him?' And there the matter ended; but it should be borne in mind that the fighting cock of a Malay Prince is not to be lightly trifled with.

I have said that all birds fight more or less, but birds are not alone in this. The little wide-mouthed, goggled-eyed fishes, which Malay ladies keep in bottles and old kerosine tins, fight like demons. Goats sit up and strike with their cloven hoofs, and butt and stab with their horns. The silly sheep canter gaily to the battle, deliver thundering blows on one another's foreheads, and then retire and charge once more. The impact of their horny foreheads is sufficient to reduce a man's hand to a shapeless pulp, should it find its way between the combatants' skulls. Tigers box like pugilists, and bite like French school-boys; and buffaloes fight clumsily, violently, and vindictively, after the manner of their kind.

The natives of India have an ingenious theory, whereby they account for the existence of that ungainly fowl, the water-buffalo,—a fact in natural history, which certainly seems to call for some explanation. The

High Gods, they say, when creating all things, made also the cow, the highest of the beasts that perish. This the devil beheld, and, in futile emulation, striving to outdo the work of the High Ones, he imitated their creation, and produced the water-buffalo! Every one who knows this brute, must admit that the Indian theory bears on its face the imprint of truth; for a more detestable beast of the field does not exist, and it would be difficult, for any one less skilled in evil than His Satanic Majesty, to have conceived the idea of so diabolical an animal. In the Malay Peninsula, its principal functions would appear to be stamping bridle-paths into quagmires; dragging unwieldy lumbering carts, and thereby frightening horses into fits; tugging and frequently running away with, all manner of primitive ploughs and sledges; and humiliating as publicly as possible, any white man that it does not gore. It seems to cherish a peculiar spite against all Europeans; for a buffalo, that is as mild as a lamb with the most unattractive native, cannot be brought to tolerate the proximity of the most refined, and least repulsive of white men. Which one is there amongst us, who does not bear a grudge against the water-buffalo as a class, and against some one black or pink bully in particular? Which of us is there, who has not passed moments in the company of these brutes, such as might well 'score years from a strong man's life'? Some of us have been gored by the brutes, and most of us, who have pursued the crafty snipe bird in his native *pâdi* swamps, have put in various *mauvais quarts d'heure*, with some of these sullenly vindictive animals mouching after us, much in the way that a *gendarme* pursues a *gamin*. Then has entered upon the scene a Delivering Angel, in the shape of a very small, very muddy, very naked child of exceedingly tender years. This tiny *deus ex machina* has straightway tackled the angry monster, with all the fearlessness of a child, has struck it twice in the face, in a most business-like manner, has piped '*Diam!* *Diam!*'[1]—which sounds like a curse word,—in a furious voice, and finally has hooked his finger into the beast's nose ring, and has led it away reluctant, and crestfallen, but unresisting. Most of us, I say, have experienced these things at the hands of the small boy and the water-buffalo; and, when both have disappeared in the brushwood, and the sweat of fear has had time to dry on our clammy foreheads, we have one and all cursed the Devil who made the brute, and have felt not a little humiliated at the superiority of the minute native boy over our wretched and abject selves.

All these bitter memories crowd into our minds, when we find ourselves in a Malay bull-ring, and we should be more than human if we felt any keen sympathy for the combatant buffaloes. We are apt to experience also an intense sense of relief at the thought that the brutes are about to fight one another, and will be too busy to waste any of their energies in persecuting the European spectators, with the amiable intention of putting them to the shame of open shame, and generally taking a rise out of them.

The bulls have been trained and medicined, for months beforehand, with much careful tending, many

---

[1] *Diam!* = Be still!

strength-giving potions, and volumes of the old-world charms, which put valour and courage into a beast. They stand at each end of a piece of grassy lawn, with their knots of admirers around them, descanting on their various points, and with the proud trainer, who is at once keeper and medicine man, holding them by the cord which is passed through their nose-rings. Until you have seen the water-buffalo stripped for the fight, it is impossible to conceive how handsome the ugly brute can look. One has been accustomed to see him with his neck bowed to the yoke he hates, and breaks whenever the opportunity offers; or else in the *pâdi* fields. In the former case he looks out of place,—an anachronism belonging to a prehistoric period, drawing a cart which seems also to date back to the days before the Deluge. In the fields the buffalo has usually a complete suit of grey mud, and during the quiet evening hour, goggles at you through the clouds of flies, which surround his flapping ears and brutal nose, the only parts that can be seen of him, above the surface of the mud-hole, or the running water of the river. In both cases he is unlovely, but in the bull-ring he has something magnificent about him. His black coat has a gloss upon it which would not disgrace a London carriage horse, and which shews him to be in tip-top condition. His neck seems thicker and more powerful than that of any other animal, and it glistens with the *chili* water, which has been poured over it, in order to increase his excitement. His resolute shoulders, his straining quarters,—each vying with the other for the prize for strength,—and his great girth, give a look of astonishing vigour and vitality to the animal. It is the head of the buffalo, however, which it is best to look at on these occasions. Its great spread of horns is very imposing, and the eyes which are usually sleepy, cynically contemptuous and indifferent, or sullenly cruel,—are for once full of life, anger, passion, and excitement. He stands there quivering and stamping, blowing great clouds of smoke from his mouth and nose:

> With his nostrils like pits full of blood to the brim.
> And with circles of red for his eye-socket's rim.

The wild joy of battle is sending the blood boiling through the great arteries of the beast, and his accustomed lethargic existence is galvanised into a new fierce life. You can see that he is longing for the battle, with an ardour that would have distanced that of a Quixote, and, for the first time, you begin to see something to admire even in the water-buffalo.

A crowd of *Râjas*, Chiefs, and commoners are assembled, in their gaily coloured garments, which always serve to give life and beauty to every Malay picture, with its setting of brilliant never-fading green. The women in their gaudy silks, and dainty veils, glance coquettishly from behind the fenced enclosure, which has been prepared for their protection, and where they are quite safe from injury. The young *Râjas* stalk about, examine the bulls, and give loud and contradictory orders, as to the manner in which the fight is to be conducted. The keepers, fortunately, are so deafened by the row which every one near them is making, that they are utterly incapable of following directions which they cannot hear. Malays love many people, and many things, and one of the latter is the sound of their own voices. When they are excited—and in the bull-ring they are always wild with excitement—they wax very noisy indeed, and, as they all talk, and no one listens to what any one else is saying, the green sward, on which the combat is to take place, speedily becomes a pandemonium, compared with which the Tower of Babel was a quiet corner in Sleepy Hollow.

At last the word to begin is given, and the keepers of the buffaloes let out the lines made fast to the bull's noses, and lead their charges to the centre of the green. The lines are crossed, and then gradually drawn taut, so that the bulls are soon facing one another. Then the knots are loosed, and the cords slip from the nose-rings. A dead silence falls upon the people, and for a moment the combatants eye one another. Then they rush together, forehead to forehead, with a mighty impact. A fresh roar rends the sky, the backers of each beast shrieking advice, and encouragement to the bull which carries their money.

After the first rush, the bulls no longer charge, but stand with interlaced horns, straining shoulders, and quivering quarters, bringing tremendous pressure to bear one upon the other, while each strives to get a grip with the point of its horns upon the neck, or cheeks, or face of its opponent. A buffalo's horn is not sharp, but the weight of the animal is enormous, and you must remember that the horns are driven with the whole of the brute's bulk for lever and sledge-hammer. Such force as is exerted, would be almost sufficient to push a crowbar through a stone wall, and, tough though they are, the hardest of old bull buffaloes is not proof against the terrible pressure brought to bear. The bulls show wonderful activity and skill in these fencing matches. Each beast gives way the instant that it is warned by the touch of the horn-tip that its opponent has found an opening, and woe betide the bull that puts its weight into a stab which the other has time to elude. In the flick of an eye,— as the Malay phrase has it,—advantage is taken of the blunder, and, before the bull has time to recover its lost balance, its opponent has found an opening, and has wedged its horn-point into the neck or cheek. When at last a firm grip has been won, and the horn has been driven into the yielding flesh, as far as the struggles of its opponent render possible, the stabber makes his great effort. Pulling his hind legs well under him, and straightening his fore-legs to the utmost extent, till the skin is drawn taut over the projecting bosses of bone at the shoulders, and the knots of muscle stand out like cordage on a crate, he lifts his opponent. His head is skewed on one side, so that the horn on which his adversary is hooked, is raised to the highest level possible, and his massive neck strains and quivers with the tremendous effort. If the stab is sufficiently low down, say in the neck, or under the cheek-bone, the wounded bull is often lifted clean off his fore-feet, and hangs there helpless and motionless 'while a man might count a score.' The exertion of lifting, however, is too great to admit of its being continued for any length of time, and as soon as the wounded buffalo regains its power of motion,—that is to say, as soon as its fore-feet are again on the ground,—it speedily releases itself from its adversary's horn. Then, since the latter is often spent, by the extraordinary effort which has been made, it frequently happens that it is stabbed, and lifted in its turn, before balance has been completely recovered.

Once, and only once, have I seen a bull succeed in throwing his opponent, after he had lifted it off its feet. The vanquished bull turned over on its back, before it succeeded in regaining its feet, but the victor was itself too used up, to more than make a ghost of a stab at the exposed stomach of its adversary. This throw is still spoken of in Pahang as the most marvellous example of skill and strength, which has ever been called forth, within living memory, by any of these contests.

As the stabs follow one another, to the sound of the clicking of the horns, and the mighty blowing and snorting of the breathless bulls, lift succeeds lift with amazing rapidity. The green turf is stamped into mud, by the great hoofs of the labouring brutes, and at length one bull owns himself to be beaten. Down goes his head,—that sure sign of exhaustion,—and in a moment, he has turned round, and is off in a bee-line, hotly pursued by the victor. The chase is never a long one, as the conqueror always abandons it at the end of a few hundred yards, but while it lasts, it is fast and furious, and woe betide the man who finds himself in the way of either of the excited animals.

Mr. Kipling has told us all about the Law of the Jungle,—which after all is only the code of man, adapted to the use of the beasts, by Mr. Rudyard Kipling,—but those who know the ways of buffaloes, are aware that they possess one very well recognised law. This is 'Thou shalt not commit trespass.' Every buffalo-bull has his own ground; and into this no other bull willingly comes. If he is brought there to do battle, he fights with very little heart, and is easily vanquished by an opponent of half his strength and bulk, who happens to be fighting on his own land. When bulls are equally matched, they are taken to fight on neutral ground. When they are badly matched, the land owned by the weaker is selected for the scene of the contest. This is an interesting fact, in its way, as it tends to prove that it is not only the unhappy Malay of Malacca who feels that he is born possessing some rights in the soil from which he springs, and on which he lives, moves, and has his being.

All these fights are brutal, and in time they will, we trust, be made illegal. To pass a prohibitionary regulation, however, without the full consent of the Chiefs and people of Pahang, would be a distinct breach of the understanding on which British Protection was accepted by them. The Government is pledged not to interfere with native customs, and the sports in which animals are engaged are among the most cherished institutions of the people of Pahang. To fully appreciate the light in which any interference with these things would be viewed by the native population, it is necessary to put oneself in the position of a keen member of the Quorn, who saw Parliament making hunting illegal, on the grounds that the sufferings inflicted on the fox, rendered it an inhuman pastime. As I have said in a former chapter, the natives of Pahang are, in their own way, very keen sportsmen indeed; and, when all is said and done, it is doubtful whether hunting is not more cruel than anything which takes place in a Malay cock-pit or bull-ring. The longer the run, the better the sport, and more intense and prolonged the agony of the fox, that strives to run for his life, even when he is so stiff with exertion, that he can do little more than roll along. All of us have, at one time or another, experienced in nightmares, the agony of attempting to fly from some pursuing phantom, when our limbs refuse to serve us. This, I fancy, is much what a fox suffers, only his pains are intensified by the grimness of stern reality. If he stops, he loses his life, therefore he rolls, and flounders, and creeps along when every movement has become a fresh torture. The cock, quail, dove, bull, ram, or fish, on the other hand, fights because it is his nature to do so, and when he has had his fill he stops. His pluck, his pride, and his hatred of defeat alone urge him to continue the contest. He is never driven by the relentless whip of stern inexorable necessity. This it is which makes fights between animals, that are properly conducted, less cruel than one is apt to imagine.

The necessity that knows no law, is the only real slave driver, as the sojourner in Eastern exile knows full well. No fetters ever gall so much, as the knowledge that the chain is made fast at the other end.

THE WERE-TIGER

Soul that is dead ere life be sped,
  Body that's body of Beast,
With brain of a man to dare and to plan,
  So make I ready my Feast!

With tooth and claw and grip of jaw
  I rip and tear and slay,
With senses that hear the winds ere they stir,
  I roam to the dawn of day.

Soul that must languish in endless anguish,
  Thy life is a little spell,
So take thy fill, ere the Pow'rs of Ill
  Shall drag Thee, Soul, to Hell.
        The Song of the Loup Garou.

IF you ask that excellent body of *savants* the Society for Psychical Research, for an opinion on the subject, they will tell you that the belief in ghosts, magic, witchcraft, and the like having existed in all ages, and in every land, is in itself a fact sufficient to warrant a faith in these things, and to establish a strong probability of their reality. It is not for me, or such as I am, to question the opinion of these wise men of the West, but if ghosts, and phantoms, and witchcraft and hag-ridings are to be accepted on such grounds, I must be allowed to put in a plea, for similar reasons, in favour of the Loup Garou, the Were-Tiger, and all their gruesome family. Wherever there are wild beasts to prey upon the sons of men, there also is found the belief that the worst and most rapacious of the man-eaters are themselves human beings, who have been driven to temporarily assume the form of an animal, by the aid of the Black Art, in order to satisfy their overpowering lust for blood. This belief, which seeks to account for the extraordinary rapacity of an animal by tracing its origin to a human being, would seem to be based upon an extremely cynical appreciation of the blood-thirsty character of our race. The white man and the brown, the yellow and the black, independently, and without receiving the idea from one another, have all found the same explanation for the like phenomena, all apparently recognising the truth of the Malay proverb, that we are like unto the *tôman* fish that preys upon its own kind. This general opinion, which seems the more worthy of acceptance in that it is the reverse of flattering to the very races that have formed this curious estimate of their own unlovely character, might by the ignorant and vulgar be supposed to be the real basis of the belief of which I speak, were it not for that dictum of the Society for Psychical Research to which I have above referred. But bowing to this authority, we must accept the Loup Garou and all its kith and kin as stern realities, and not attribute it, as we might perhaps have been inclined to do, to a deadly fear of wild beasts, coupled to a thorough knowledge of the unpleasant qualities of primitive human nature.

Educated Europeans, who live in a land where even

Nature, when she can be seen for the houses, has had man's hall-mark scarred deep into her face, are apt to think that the Age of Superstition has gone to fill the lumber-room of the past. Occasionally they are awakened from this belief by the torturing of a witch in a cabin by an Irish-bog; but even an event so near home as that is powerless to altogether disabuse their minds of their preconceived opinion. The difficulty really is, that they cannot get completely rid of the notion that the world is peopled by educated Europeans like themselves, and by a few other unimportant persons, who do not matter. They know that, numerically, they are as but a drop in the ocean of mankind, but it is possible to know a thing very thoroughly and to realise it not at all. Thus they come by their false opinion; for, in truth, the Age of Superstition lives as lustily to-day, as when, in past years, witches blazed at Smithfield, or died with rending gulps and bursting lungs, lashed fast to an English ducking stool.

In the remote portions of the Malay Peninsula we live in the Middle Ages, with all the appropriate accessories of the dark centuries. Magic and evil spirits, witchcraft and sorcery, spells and love-potions, charms and incantations are, to the mind of the native, as real and as much a matter of everyday life as are the miracle of the growing rice, and the mysteries of the reproduction of species. This must be not only known but realised, not only accepted as a theory, but acknowledged as a fact, if the native view of life is to be understood and appreciated. Tales of the marvellous and the supernatural excite interest and fear in a Malay audience, but they occasion no surprise. Malays know that strange things have happened in the past, and are daily occurring to them and to their fellows. Some are struck by lightning, while others go unscathed; and similarly some have strange experiences, which are not wholly of this world, while others live and die untouched by the supernatural. The two cases, to the Malay mind, are completely parallel; and though both furnish matter for discussion, and excite fear and awe, neither are unheard of phenomena calculated to awaken wonder and surprise.

Thus the existence of the Malayan Loup Garou to the native mind is a fact and not a mere belief. The Malay *knows* that it is true. Evidence, if it be needed, may be had in plenty; the evidence, too, of soberminded men, whose words, in a Court of Justice, would bring conviction to the mind of the most obstinate jurymen, and be more than sufficient to hang the most innocent of prisoners. The Malays know well how Haji Äbdallah, the native of the little state of Korinchi in Sumatra, was caught naked in a tiger trap, and thereafter purchased his liberty at the price of the buffaloes he had slain, while he marauded in the likeness of a beast. They know of the countless Korinchi men who have vomited feathers, after feasting upon fowls, when for the nonce they had assumed the forms of tigers; and of those other men of the same race who have left their garments and their trading packs in thickets, whence presently a tiger has emerged. All these things the Malays know have happened, and are happening to-day, in the land in which they live, and with these plain evidences before their eyes, the empty assurances of the enlightened European that Were-

Tigers do not, and never did exist, excite derision not unmingled with contempt.

The Slim Valley lies across the hills which divide Pahang from Pêrak. It is peopled by Malays of various races. Râwas and Měnangkâbaus from Sumatra, men with high-sounding titles and vain boasts, wherewith to carry off their squalid, dirty poverty; Pêrak men from the fair Kinta valley, prospecting for tin, or trading skilfully; fugitives from Pahang, long settled in the district; and the sweepings of Sumatra, Java, and the Peninsula. It was in this place that I heard the following story of a Were-Tiger, from Pěnghûlu Mat Saleh, who was, and perhaps is still, the Headman of this miscellaneous crew.

Into the Slim Valley, some years ago, there came a Korinchi trader named Haji Äli, and his two sons, Äbdulrahman and Äbas. They came, as is the manner of their people, laden with heavy packs of *sárongs*,—the native skirts or waist-cloths,—trudging in single file through the forests and through the villages, hawking their goods to the natives of the place, with much cunning haggling or hard bargaining. But though they came to trade, they stayed long after the contents of their packs had been disposed of, for Haji Äli took a fancy to the place. Therefore he presently purchased a compound, and with his two sons set to work upon planting cocoa nuts, and cultivating a rice-swamp. They were quiet, well-behaved people; they were regular in their attendance at the mosque for the Friday congregational prayers, and as they were wealthy and prosperous they found favour in the eyes of their poorer neighbours. Thus it happened that when Haji Äli let it be known that he desired to find a wife, there was a bustle in the villages among the parents with marriageable daughters, and, though he was a man well past middle life, Haji Äli found a wide range of choice offered to him.

The girl he selected was Patîmah, the daughter of poor parents, peasants living on their land in one of the neighbouring villages. She was a comely maiden, plump and round, and light of colour, with a merry face to cheer, and willing fingers wherewith to serve a husband. The wedding portion was paid, a feast proportionate to Haji Äli's wealth was held to celebrate the occasion, and the bride was carried off, after a decent interval, to her husband's home among the fruit groves and the palm-trees. This was not the general custom of the land, for among Malays the husband usually shares his father-in-law's house for a long period after his marriage. But Haji Äli had a fine new house of his own, brave with wattled walls stained cunningly in black and white, and with a luxuriant covering of thatch. Moreover, he had taken the daughter of a poor man to wife, and could dictate his own terms to her and to her parents. The girl went willingly enough, for she was exchanging poverty for wealth, a miserable hovel for a handsome home, and parents who knew exactly how to get out of her the last fraction of work of which she was capable, for a husband who seemed ever kind, generous, and indulgent. None the less, three days later she was found beating on the door of her parents' house, at the hour when dawn was breaking, trembling in every limb, with her hair disordered, her garments drenched with dew from the brushwood through which she had forced her way, with her eyes wild with horror, and mad with a great fear. Her story—the first act in the drama of the Were-Tiger of Slim—ran in this wise, though I shall not attempt to reproduce the words or the manner in which she told it, brokenly, with shuddering ṣobs, to her awe-stricken parents.

She had gone home with Haji Äli to the house where he dwelt with his two sons, Äbdulrahman and Äbas, and all had treated her kindly and with courtesy. The first day she cooked the rice ill, but though the young men grumbled, Haji Äli said never a word of blame, when she had expected blows, such as would have fallen to the lot of most wives under similar circumstances. She had no complaint to make of her husband's kindness, but none the less she had fled his dwelling, and her parents might 'hang her on high, sell her in a far land, scorch her with the sun's rays, immerse her in water, burn her with fire,' but never again would she return to one who hunted by night as a Were-Tiger.

Every evening after the Ïsa[1] Haji Äli had left the house on one pretext or another, and had not returned until an hour before the dawn. Twice she had not been aware of his return until she found him lying on the sleeping-mat by her side; but, on the third evening, she had remained awake until a noise without told her that her husband was at hand. Then she had hastened to unbar the door, which she had fastened after Äbas and Äbdulrahman had fallen asleep. The moon was behind a cloud, and the light she cast was

[1] Ïsa = The hour of evening prayer.

dim, but Patîmah saw clearly enough the sight which had driven her mad with terror.

On the topmost rung of the ladder, which in this, as in all Malay houses, led from the ground to the threshold of the door, there rested the head of a full-grown tiger. Patîmah could see the bold, black stripes which marked his hide, the bristling wires of whisker, the long cruel teeth, and the fierce green light in the beast's eyes. A round pad, with long curved claws partially concealed, lay on the ladder rung, one on each side of the monster's head, and the lower portion of its body reaching to the ground was so foreshortened that to the girl it looked like the body of a man. Patîmah gazed at the tiger, from the distance of only a foot or two, for she was too paralysed with fear to move or cry out, and as she looked a gradual transformation took place in the creature at her feet. Slowly, as one sees a ripple of wind pass over the surface of still water, the tiger's features palpitated and were changed, until the horrified girl saw the face of her husband come up through that of the beast, much as the face of a diver comes up to the surface of a pool. In another moment Patîmah saw that it was Haji Äli who was ascending the ladder of his house, and the spell that had hitherto bound her was snapped. The first use she made of her regained power of motion was to leap through the doorway past her husband, and to plunge into the jungle which edged the compound.

Malays do not love to travel singly through the jungle even when the sun is high, and under ordinary circumstances no woman could by any means be prevailed upon to do such a thing. But Patîmah was wild with fear of what she had left behind her, and though she was alone, though the moonlight was dim, and the dawn had not yet come, she preferred the dismal depths of the forest to the home of her Were-Tiger husband. Thus she pushed her way through the underwood, tearing her garments and her flesh with thorns, catching her feet in creepers and trailing vines, stumbling over unseen logs, and drenching herself to the skin with the dew from the leaves and grasses against which she brushed. A little before daybreak she made her way, as I have described, to her father's house, there to tell the tale of her strange adventure.

The story of what had occurred was speedily noised through the villages, and the parents with marriageable daughters, who had been disappointed by Haji Äli's choice of a wife, rejoiced exceedingly, and did not forget to tell Patîmah's papa and mamma that they had always anticipated something of the sort. Haji Äli made no effort to regain possession of his wife, and his neighbours drawing a natural inference from his actions, avoided him and his sons until they were forced to live in almost complete isolation.

But the drama of the Were-Tiger of Slim was to have a final act.

One night a fine young water-buffalo, the property of the Headman, Pĕnghûlu Mat Saleh, was killed by a tiger, and its owner, saying no word to any man upon the subject, constructed a cunningly arranged spring-gun over the carcase. The trigger-lines were so set that should the tiger return to finish the meal, which he had begun by tearing a couple of hurried mouthfuls from the rump of his kill, he must infallibly be wounded or slain by the bolts and slugs with which the gun was charged.

Next night a loud report, breaking in clanging echoes through the stillness, an hour or two before the dawn was due, apprised Pĕnghûlu Mat Saleh that some animal had fouled the trigger-lines. In all probability it was the tiger, and if he was wounded he would not be a pleasant creature to meet on a dark night. Accordingly Pĕnghûlu Mat Saleh lay still until morning.

In a Malay village all are astir very shortly after daybreak. As soon as it is light enough to see to walk the doors of the houses open one by one, and the people of the village come forth singly huddled to the chin in their *sârongs* or bed coverlets. Each man makes his way down to the river to perform his morning ablutions, or stands on the bank of the stream, staring sleepily at nothing in particular, a black figure silhouetted against the broad ruddiness of a Malayan dawn. Presently the women of the village come out of the houses, in little knots of three or four, with the children pattering at their heels. They carry clusters of gourds in either hand, for it is their duty to fill them from the running stream with the water which will be needed during the day. It is not until the sun begins to rise, when morning ablutions have been carefully performed, and the first sleepiness of the waking hour has departed from heavy eyes, that the people of the village begin to set about the avocations of the day.

Pĕnghûlu Mat Saleh arose that morning and performed his usual daily routine before he collected a party of Malays to aid him in his search for the wounded tiger. He had no difficulty in finding men who were willing to share the excitement of the adventure, and presently he set off with a ragged following of near a dozen at his heels, the party having two guns and many spears and *kris*. They reached the spot where the spring-gun had been set, and they found that beyond a doubt the tiger had returned to his kill. The tracks left by the great pads were fresh, and the tearing up of the earth on one side of the dead buffalo, in a spot where the grass was thickly flecked with blood, showed that the shot had taken effect.

Pĕnghûlu Mat Saleh and his people then set down steadily to follow the trail of the wounded tiger. This was an easy matter, for the beast had gone heavily on three legs, the off-hind leg dragging uselessly. In places, too, a clot of blood showed red among the dew-drenched leaves and grasses. None the less the Pĕnghûlu and his party followed slowly and with caution. They knew that a wounded tiger is never in a mood in which a child may play with him, and also that, even when he has only three legs with which to spring upon his enemies, he can on occasion arrange for a large escort of human beings to accompany him into the land of shadows.

The trail led through the brushwood, in which the dead buffalo lay, and thence into a belt of jungle which edged the river bank a few hundred yards above Pĕnghûlu Mat Saleh's village, and extended up-stream to Kuâla Chin Lâma, a distance of half a dozen miles. The tiger turned up-stream when this jungle was reached, and half a mile higher up he came out upon a slender wood-path.

When Pĕnghûlu Mat Saleh had followed thus far, he halted and looked at his people.

'Know ye whither this track leads, my brothers?' he asked in a whisper.

The men nodded, but said never a word. A glance at them would have shown you that they were anxious and uneasy.

'What say ye?' continued the Pĕnghûlu. 'Do we still follow this trail?'

'It is as thou wilt, O Pĕnghûlu,' said the oldest man of the party, answering for his fellows, 'we follow thee whithersoever thou goest.'

'It is well!' said the Pĕnghûlu. 'Come let us go.' No more was said, when this whispered colloquy was ended, and the party set down to the trail again silently and with redoubled caution.

The narrow track, which the wounded tiger had followed, led on towards the river bank, and presently the high wattled bamboo fence of a native compound became visible through the trees. Pĕnghûlu Mat Saleh pointed at it. 'Behold!' was all he said. Then the party moved on again, still following the tracks of the tiger, and the flecks of red blood on the grass. These led them to the gate of the compound, and through it to the *'lâman* or open space before the house. Here they were lost at a spot where the rank spear-blades of the *lâlang* grass had been beaten down by the falling of some heavy body. A veritable pool of blood marked the place. To it the trail of the limping tiger led. Away from it there was no tracks, save those of the human beings who come and go through the rank growths which cloak the earth in a Malay compound.

'Behold!' said Pĕnghûlu Mat Saleh once more. 'Come, let us ascend into the house.' And so saying he led the way up the stair-ladder of the dwelling where Haji Äli lived with his two sons Äbas and Äbdulrahman, and whence a month or two before Patîmah had fled during the night-time with a deadly fear in her eyes, and the tale of a strange experience faltering on her lips.

Pĕnghûlu Mat Saleh and his people found Äbas sitting cross-legged in the outer apartment preparing a quid of betel-nut with elaborate care. The visitors squatted on the mats, and the usual customary salutations over, Pĕnghûlu Mat Saleh said:

'I have come in order that I may see thy father. Is he within the house?'

'He is,' said Äbas laconically.

'Then make known to him that I would have speech with him.'

'My father is sick,' said Äbas in a surly tone, and at the word a tremor of excitement ran through Pĕnghûlu Mat Saleh's followers.

'What is that patch of blood in the *lâlang* before the house?' asked the Pĕnghûlu conversationally, after a short pause.

'We slew a goat yesternight,' replied Äbas.

'Hast thou the skin, O Äbas?' asked the Pĕnghûlu, 'for I am renewing the faces of my drums, and would fain purchase it.'

'The skin was mangy, and we cast it into the river,' said Äbas.

'What ails thy father, Äbas?' asked the Pĕnghûlu returning to the charge.

'He is sick,' said suddenly a voice from the curtained doorway, which led to the inner apartment. It was the elder son Äbdulrahman who spoke. He held a sword in his hand, and his face wore an ugly look as his words came harshly and gratingly with the foreign accent of the Korinchi people. He went on, still standing, near the doorway, 'He is sick, O Pênghûlu, and the noise of your words disturbs him. He would slumber and be still. Descend out of the house, he cannot see thee, Pĕnghûlu. Listen to these my words!'

Äbdulrahman's manner, and the words he spoke, were at once so rough and defiant that the Pĕnghûlu saw that he must choose between a scuffle, which would mean bloodshed, and a hasty retreat. He was a mild old man, and he drew a monthly salary from the Pĕrak Government. Moreover, he knew that the white men, who guided the destinies of Pĕrak, were averse to bloodshed and homicide, even if the person slain was a wizard, or the son of a wizard. Therefore he decided upon retreat.

As they clambered down the steps of the doorladder, Mat Tahir, one of the Pĕnghûlu's men, plucked him by the sleeve, and pointed to a spot beneath the house. Just below the place, in the inner apartment, where Haji Äli might be supposed to lie stretched upon the mat of sickness, the ground was stained a dim red for a space of several inches in circumference. Malay floors are made of laths of wood or of bamboo laid parallel to one another, with spaces between each one of them. This is convenient, as the whole of the ground beneath the house can thus be used as a slop-pail, waste-basket, and rubbish heap. The red stain lying where it did had the look of blood, blood moreover from some one within the house, whose wound had very recently been washed and dressed. It might also have been the red juice of the betel-nut, but its stains are but rarely seen in such large patches. Whatever it may have been the Pĕnghûlu and his people had no opportunity of examining it more closely, for Äbdulrahman and Äbas followed them out of the compound, and barred the door against them.

Then the Pĕnghûlu set off to tell his tale to the District Officer, the white man under whose charge the Slim Valley had been placed. He went with many misgivings, for Europeans are sceptical concerning such tales, and when he returned, more or less dissatisfied, some five days later, he found that Haji Äli and his sons had disappeared. They had fled down river on a dark night, without a soul being made aware of their intended departure. They had neither stayed to reap their crops, which now stood ripening in the fields; to sell their house and compound, which had been bought with good money,—'dollars of the whitest,' as the Malay phrase has it,—nor yet to collect their debts. This is a fact; and to one who knows the passion for wealth and for property, which is to be found in the breast of every Sumatran Malay, it is perhaps the strangest circumstance of all the weird events, which go to make up the drama of the Were-Tiger of Slim.

There is, to the European mind, only one possible explanation. Haji Äli and his sons had been the victims of foul play. They had been killed by the simple villagers of Slim, and a cock-and-bull story trumped up to account for their disappearance. This is a very good, and withal a very astute explanation, showing as it does a profound knowledge of human nature, and I should be more than half inclined to accept it as the correct one, but for the fact that Haji Äli and his sons turned up in quite another part of the Peninsula some months later. They have nothing out of the way about them to mark them from their fellows, except that Haji Äli goes lame on his right leg.

THE ÂMOK OF DÂTO KÂYA BÎJI DĔRJA

> I have done for ever with all these things,
> —Deeds that were joyous to knights and kings,
>   In the days that with song were cherish'd.
> The songs are ended, the deeds are done,
> There's none shall gladden me now, not one,
> There is nothing good for me under the sun,
>   But to perish as these things perish'd.
> The Rhyme of the Joyous Garde.

THE average stay-at-home Englishman knows very little about the Malay, and cares less. Any fragmentary ideas that he may have concerning him are, for the most part, vague and hopelessly wrong. When he thinks of him at all, which is not often, he conjures up the figure of a wild-eyed, long-haired, blood-smeared, howling and naked savage, armed with what Tennyson calls the 'cursed Malayan crease,' who spends all his spare time running *âmok*. As a matter of fact, *âmok* are not as common as people suppose, but false ideas on the subject, and more especially concerning the reasons which lead a Malay to run *âmok*, are not confined to those Europeans who know nothing about the natives of the Peninsula. White men, in the East and out of it, are apt to attribute *âmok* running to madness pure and simple, and, as such, to regard it as a form of disease, to which any Malay is liable, and which is as involuntary on his part as an attack of smallpox. This, I venture to think, is a mistaken view of the matter. It is true that some *âmok* are caused by madness, but such acts are not peculiar to the Malays. Given a lunatic who has arms always within his reach, and the result is likely to be the same, no matter what the land in which he lives, or the race to which he belongs. In independent Malay States everybody goes about armed; and weapons, therefore, are always available. As a consequence, madmen often run *âmok*, but such cases are not typical, and do not present any of the characteristic features which distinguish the *âmok* among Malays, from similar acts committed by people of other nationalities. By far the greater number of Malay *âmok* results from a condition of mind which is described in the vernacular by the term *sâkit hâti*—sickness of liver—that organ, and not the heart, being regarded as the centre of sensibility. The states of feeling which are described by this phrase are numerous, complex, and differ widely in degree, but they all imply some measure of anger, excitement, and mental irritation. A Malay loses something he values; he has a bad night in the gambling houses; some of his property is wantonly damaged; he has a quarrel with one whom he loves; his father dies; or his mistress proves unfaithful; any one of these things causes him 'sickness of liver.' In the year 1888, I spent two nights awake by the side of Râja Haji Hamid, with difficulty restraining him from running *âmok* in the streets of Pĕkan, because his father had died a natural death in Sĕlângor. He had no quarrel with the people of Pahang, but his 'liver was sick,' and to run *âmok* was, in his opinion, the natural remedy. This is merely one instance of many which might be cited, and serves to illustrate my contention that *âmok* is caused, in most cases, by a condition of mind, which may result from either serious or comparatively trivial causes, but which, while it lasts, makes a native weary of life. At such times, he is doubtless to some extent a madman—just as all suicides are more or less insane—but the state of feeling which drives a European to take his own life makes a Malay run *âmok*. All Malays have the greatest horror of suicide, and I know of no properly authenticated case in which a male Malay has committed such an act, but I have known several who ran *âmok* when a white man, under similar circumstances, would not improbably have taken his own life. Often enough something trivial begins the trouble, and, in the heat of the moment, a blow is struck by a man against one whom he holds dear, and the hatred of self which results, causes him to long for death, and to seek it in the only way which occurs to a Malay— namely, by running *âmok*. A man who runs *âmok*, too, almost always kills his wife. He is anxious to die himself, and he sees no reason why his wife should survive him, and, in a little space, become the property of some other man. He also frequently destroys his most valued possessions, as they have become useless to him, since he cannot take them with him to that bourne whence no traveller returns. The following story, for the truth of which I can vouch in every particular, illustrates all that I have said :

THE ÂMOK OF DÀTO KÂYA BÎJI DĔRJA

In writing of the natives of the East Coast, I have mentioned that the people of Trĕnggânu are, first and foremost, men of peace. This must be borne in mind in reading what follows, for I doubt whether things could have fallen out as they did in any other Native State, and, at the time when these events occurred, the want of courage and skill shown by the Trĕnggânu people made them the laughing stock of the whole of the East Coast. To this day no Trĕnggânu man likes to be chaffed about the doings of his countrymen at the *âmok* of Biji Dĕrja, and any reference to it, gives as much offence as does the whisper of the magic words 'Rusty buckles' in the ears of the men of a certain cavalry regiment.

When Bâginda Ŭmar ruled in Trĕnggânu there was a Chief named To' Bĕntàra Haji, who was one of the monarch's adopted sons, and early in the present reign the eldest son of this Chief was given the title of Dàto' Kâya Bîji Dĕrja. At this, the minds of the good people of Trĕnggânu were not a little exercised, for the title is one which it is not usual to confer upon a commoner, and Jûsup, the man now selected to bear it, was both young and untried. He was of no particular birth, he possessed no book-learning—such as the Trĕnggânu people love—and was not even skilled in the warrior's lore which is so highly prized by the ruder natives of Pahang. The new To' Kâya was fully sensible of his unfitness for the post, and determined to do all that in him lay to remedy his deficiencies. He probably knew that, as a student, he could never hope to excel; so he set his heart on acquiring the *ĕlĕmu hûlubâlang*, or occult sciences,

G

which it behoves a fighting man to possess. In Trĕnggânu there were few warriors to teach him the lore he desired to learn, though he was a pupil of Tŭngku Long Pĕndêkar, who was skilled in fencing and other kindred arts. At night-time, therefore, he took to haunting graveyards, in the hope that the ghosts of the mighty dead—the warriors of ancient times—would appear to him and instruct him in the sciences which had died with them.

Women are notoriously perverse, and To' Kâya's wife persisted in misunderstanding the motives which kept him abroad far into the night. She attributed his absences to the blandishments of some unknown lady, and she refused to be pacified by his explanations, just as other wives, in more civilised communities, have obstinately disregarded the excuses of their husbands, when the latter have pleaded that 'business' has detained them.

At length, for the sake of peace and quietness, To' Kâya abandoned his nocturnal prowls among the graves, and settled down to live the orderly domestic life for which he was best fitted, and which he had only temporarily forsaken when the Sultân's ill-advised selection of him to fill a high post, and to bear a great name, had interrupted the even tenor of his ways.

One day, his father, To' Bĕntâra Haji, fell sick, and was removed to the house of one Che' Äli, a medicine man of some repute. To' Kâya was a dutiful son, and he paid many visits to his father in his sickness, tending him unceasingly, and consequently he did not return to his home until late at night. I have said that this was an old cause of offence, and angry recriminations passed between him and his wife, which were only made more bitter because To' Kâya mistook a stringy piece of egg, in his wife's sweetmeats, for a human hair. To a European, this does not sound a very important matter, but To' Kâya, in common with many Malays, believed that a hair in his food betokened that the dish was poisoned, and he refused to touch it, hinting that his wife desired his death. Next night he was also absent until a late hour, tending his father in his sickness, and, on his return, his wife again abused him for infidelity to her. He cried to her to unbar the door, which, at length, she did, using many injurious words the while, and he, in his anger, replied that he would shortly have to stab her to teach her better manners.

At this she flew into a perfect fury of rage, 'Hei! Stab then! Stab!' she cried, and, as she shouted the words, she made a gesture which is the grossest insult that a Malay woman can put upon a man. At this To' Kâya lost both his head and his temper, and, hardly knowing what he did, he drew his dagger clear and she took the point in her breast, their baby, who was on her arm, being also slightly wounded. Dropping the child upon the verandah, she rushed past her husband, and took refuge in the house of a neighbour named Che' Long. To' Kâya followed her, and cried to those within the house to unbar the door. Che' Long's daughter Ësah ran to comply with his bidding; but, before she could do so, To' Kâya had crept under the house, and he stabbed at her savagely through the interstices of the bamboo flooring, wounding her in the hip. The girl's father, hearing the noise, ran out of the house, and was greeted by To' Kâya with a spear thrust in the stomach which doubled him up, and, like Abner Dean of Angel's, 'the subsequent proceedings interested him no more.' Meanwhile, To' Kâya's wife had rushed out of the house, and returned to her home. Her husband pursued her, overtook her on the verandah, and stabbed her through the breast, killing her on the spot.

He then entered his house, which was still tenanted by his son, and his mother-in-law, and set fire to the bed curtains with a box of matches. Now, the people of Kuâla Trĕnggânu dread fire more than anything in the world; for, their houses, which are made of very inflammable material, jostle one another on every foot of available ground. When a Trĕnggânu man deliberately sets fire to his own house, he has reached the highest pitch of desperation, and is 'burning his ships' in sober earnest. At the sight of the flames, To' Kâya's son, a boy of about twelve years of age, made a rush at the curtains, pulled them down, and stamped the fire out. To' Kâya's mother-in-law, meanwhile, had rushed out of the house, seized the baby who still lay on the verandah, and set off at a run. The sight of his mother-in-law in full flight was too much for To' Kâya, who probably owed her many grudges, and he at once gave chase, overtook her, and stabbed her through the shoulder. She, however, succeeded in making good her escape, carrying the baby with her. To' Kâya then returned to his house, whence his son had also fled, and set it afire once more, and this time it blazed up bravely.

As he stood looking at the flames, a Kĕlantan man

THE ÂMOK OF DÂTO KÂYA BÎJI DĔRJA

named Äbdul Rahman came up and asked him how the house had caught fire.

'I know not,' said To' Kâya.

'Let us try to save some of the property,' said Äbdul Rahman, for, like many Kĕlantan natives, he was a thief by trade, and knew that a fire gave him a good opportunity of practising his profession.

'Good!' said To' Kâya, 'Mount thee into the house, and lift the boxes, while I wait here and receive them.'

Nothing loth, Äbdul Rahman climbed into the house, and presently appeared with a large box in his arms. As he leaned over the verandah, in the act of handing it down to To' Kâya, the latter stabbed him shrewdly in the vitals, and box and man came to the ground with a crash. Äbdul Rahman picked himself up, and ran as far as the big stone mosque, where he collapsed and died. To' Kâya did not pursue him, but stood looking at the leaping flames.

The next man to arrive on the scene was Pa' Pek, a Trĕnggânu native, who, with his wife Ma' Pek, had tended To' Kâya when he was little.

'Wo',' he said, for he spoke to To' Kâya as though the latter was his son, 'Wo', what has caused this fire?'

'I know not,' said To' Kâya.

'Where are thy children, Wo'?' asked Pa' Pek.

'They are still within the house,' said To' Kâya.

'Then suffer me to save them,' said Pa' Pek.

'Do so, Pa' Pek,' said To' Kâya, and, as the old man climbed into the house, he stabbed him in the ribs, and Pa' Pek ran away towards the mosque till he tripped over the prostrate body of Äbdul Rahman, fell, and eventually died where he lay.

Presently, Ma' Pek came to look for her husband, and asked To' Kâya about the fire, and where the children were.

'They are still in the house,' said To' Kâya, 'but I cannot be bothered to take them out of it.'

'Let me fetch them,' said Ma' Pek.

'Do so, by all means,' said To' Kâya, and, as she scrambled up, he stabbed her as he had done her husband, and she, running away, tripped over the two other bodies, and gave up the ghost.

Then a Trĕnggânu boy named Jûsup came up, armed with a spear, and To' Kâya tried to kill him, but he hid behind a tree. To' Kâya at first emptied his revolver at Jûsup, missing with all six chambers, and then, throwing away the pistol, he stabbed at him with his spear, but in the darkness he struck the tree. 'Thou art invulnerable!' he cried, thinking that the tree was Jûsup's chest, and, a panic seizing him, he promptly turned and fled. Jûsup, meanwhile, made off in the opposite direction as fast as his frightened legs would carry him.

Seeing that he was not pursued, To' Kâya returned, and went to Tŭngku Long Pĕndêkar's house. At the alarm of fire, all the men in the house—Tŭngku Long, Tŭngku Itam, Tŭngku Pa, Tŭngku Chik, and Che' Mat Tŭkang—had rushed out, but all of them had gone back again to remove their effects, with the exception of Tŭngku Long himself, who stood looking at the flames. He was armed with a rattan-work shield, and an ancient and very pliable native sword. As he stood gazing upwards, quite unaware that any trouble, other than that involved by the conflagration, was toward, To' Kâya rushed upon him and stabbed him with his spear in the ribs. For a long time they fought, Tŭngku Long lashing To' Kâya with his little pliable sword, but only succeeding in bruising him. At length, To' Kâya was wounded in the left hand, and almost at the same moment he struck Tŭngku Long with such force in the centre of the shield that he knocked him down. He then jumped upon his chest, and, stabbing downwards, as one stabs fish with a spear, pinned him through the neck. Tŭngku Itam, who had been watching the struggle as men watch a cock-fight, without taking any part in it, then ran away. To' Kâya passed out of the compound, and Che' Mat Tŭkang, running out of the house, climbed up the fence and threw a spear at To' Kâya, striking him in the back. Che' Mat then very prudently ran away too.

To' Kâya, passing up the path, met a woman named Ma' Chik—a very aged, bent, and feeble crone—and her he stabbed in the breast, killing her on the spot. Thence he went to the compound of a pilgrim named Haji Mih, who was engaged in getting his property out of his house in case the fire spread. Haji Mih asked To' Kâya how the fire had originated.

'God alone knows,' said To' Kâya, and so saying, he stabbed Haji Mih through the shoulder.

'Help! Help!' cried the pilgrim, and his son-in-law Saleh and four other men rushed out of the house and fell upon To' Kâya, driving him backwards in the fight until he tripped and fell. Then, as he lay on his back, he stabbed upwards, striking Saleh through the elbow and deep into his chest. At this, Saleh and all the other men with him fled incontinently. To' Kâya, then picked himself up. He had not been hurt in the struggle, for Saleh and his people had not stayed to unbind their spears, which were fastened into bundles, and, save for the slight wounds in his hand and on his back, he was little the worse for his adventures.

He next went to the Makam Lĕbai Salâm—the grave of an ancient Saint—and here he bathed in a well hard by, dressed himself, and eat half a tin of Messrs. Huntly and Palmer's 'gem' biscuits, which he had brought with him. Having completed his toilet, he returned to Haji Mih's house and cried out:

'Where are those my enemies, who engaged me in fight a little while agone?'

It was now about 3 A.M., but the men were awake and heard him.

'Come quickly!' he shouted again, 'Come quickly, and let us finish this little business with no needless delay.'

At this, ten men rushed out of Haji Mih's house, and began to throw spears at him, but though they struck him more than once they did not succeed in wounding him. He retreated backwards, and, in doing so, he tripped over a root near a clump of bamboos and fell to the earth. Seeing this, the men fancied that they had killed him, and fear fell upon them, for he was a Chief, and they had no warrant from the Sultân. Thereupon they fled, and To' Kâya once more gathered himself together and returned to Lĕbai Salâm's grave, where he finished the tin of 'gem' biscuits.

At dawn he returned to Haji Mih's house. Here he halted to bandage his wounds with the rags of cotton that had been bound about some rolls of mats and pillows, which Haji Mih had removed from the house at the alarm of fire. Then he shouted to the men within the house to come out and fight with him anew, but no one came, and he laughed aloud and went on down the road till he came to Tŭngku Pa's house. Tŭngku Pa and a man named Sĕmäil were in the verandah, and when the alarm was raised that To' Kâya was coming, Tŭngku Pa's wife rushed to the door, and bolted it on the inside, while her husband yammered to be let in.

When To' Kâya saw him, he cried to him as he would have cried to an equal :

'O Pa ! I have waited for thee the long night through though thou camest not. I have much desired to fight with a man of rank. At last we have met, and I shall have my desire.'

Sĕmäil at once made a bolt of it, but To' Kâya was too quick for him, and as he leaped down, the spear took him through the body, and he died. Then Tŭngku Pa stabbed down at To' Kâya from the verandah and struck him in the groin, the spear head becoming bent in the muscles, so that it could not be withdrawn. Now was Tŭngku Pa's opportunity, but instead of seizing it and rushing in upon To' Kâya to finish him with his *kris*, he let go the handle of the spear, and fled to a large water jar, behind which he sought shelter. To' Kâya tugged at the spear, and at length succeeded in wrenching it free, and Tŭngku Pa, seeing this, broke cover from behind the jar, and took to his heels. To' Kâya was too lame to attempt to overtake him, but he cried out :

'He, Pa! Did the men of old bid thee fly from thy enemies ?'

Tŭngku Pa halted and turned round. 'I am only armed with a *kris*, and have no spear as thou hast,' he said.

'This house is thine,' said To' Kâya. 'If thou dost desire arms, go up into the house, and fetch as many as thou canst carry, while I await thy coming.'

But Tŭngku Pa had had enough, and he turned and fled at the top of his speed.

'Hah! Hah! Hah! Ho! Ho! Ho!' laughed To' Kâya. 'Is this, then, the manner in which the men of the rising generation fight their enemies?'

Seeing that Tŭngku Pa was in no wise to be tempted or shamed into giving battle, To' Kâya went past the spot where the body of Ma' Chik still lay, until he came to the pool of blood which marked the place where Tûngku Long Pĕndêkar had come by his death. Standing there, he cried to Tŭngku Îtam who was within the house :

'O Tŭngku! Be pleased to come forth if thou desire to avenge the death of Tŭngku Long, thy cousin. Now is the acceptable time, for thy servant has still some little life left in him. Hereafter thou mayst not avenge thy cousin's death, thy servant being dead. Condescend, therefore, to come forth and fight with thy servant.'

But Tŭngku Îtam, like Gallio, cared for none of

THE ÂMOK OF DÂTO KÂYA BÎJI DĔRJA

these things, and To' Kâya, seeing that his challenge was not answered, cried once more:

'If thou will not take vengeance, the fault is none of thy servant's,' and, so saying, he passed upon his way.

The dawn was breaking grayly, and the cool land breeze was making a little stir in the fronds of the palm trees, as To' Kâya passed up the lane, and through the compounds, whose owners had fled hastily from fear of him. Presently, he came out on the open space before the mosque, and here some four hundred men, fully armed with spears and daggers, were assembled. It was light enough for To' Kâya to see and mark the fear in their eyes. He smiled grimly.

'This is indeed good!' cried he. 'Now at last shall I have my fill of stabbing and fighting,' and, thereupon, he made a shambling, limping charge at the crowd, which wavered, broke, and fled in every direction, the majority rushing into the enclosure of Tŭngku Ngah's compound, the door of which they barred.

One of the hindermost was a man named Gĕnih, and to him To' Kâya shouted:

'O Gĕnih! it profits the *Râja* little that he gives thou and such as thee food both morning and evening! Thou art indeed a *bitter* coward.[1] If thou fearest me so greatly, go seek for guns and kill me from afar off!'

Gĕnih took To' Kâya's advice. He rushed to the *Bâlai*, or State Hall, and cried to Tŭngku Mûsa, the Sultân's uncle and principal adviser:

[1] *Pĕn-âkut pâhit.*

'Thy servant To' Kâya bids us bring guns wherewith to slay him.'

Now, all was not well in the *Bâlai* at this moment. When the first news of the *âmok* had reached the Sultân, all the Chiefs had assembled in the palace, and it had been unanimously decided that no action could be taken until the day broke. At dawn, however, it was found that all the Chiefs except Tŭngku Pănglîma, To' Kâya Dûyong, Pănglîma Dâlam, Imâm Prang Lôsong, and Pahlâwan, had sneaked away under the cover of the darkness. Tŭngku Mûsa, the Sultân's great uncle, was there to act as the King's mouthpiece, but he was in as great fear as any of them.

At last the Sultân said:

'Well, the day has dawned, why does no one go forth to kill To' Kâya Bîji Dĕrja?'

Tŭngku Mûsa turned upon Tŭngku Pănglîma, 'Go thou and slay him,' he said.

Tŭngku Pănglîma said, 'Why dost thou not go thyself or send Pahlâwan?'

Pahlâwan said, 'Thy servant is not the only Chief in Trĕnggânu. Many eat the King's mutton in the King's *Bâlai*, why then should thy servant alone be called upon to do this thing?'

Tŭngku Mûsa said: 'Imâm Prang Lôsong, go thou then and kill To' Kâya.'

'I cannot go,' said Imâm Prang, 'for I have no trousers.'

'I will give thee some trousers,' said Tŭngku Mûsa.

'Nevertheless I cannot go,' said Imâm Prang, 'for my mother is sick, and I must return to tend her.'

Then the Sultân stood upon his feet and stamped.

'What manner of a warrior is this?' he asked, pointing at Tŭngku Pănglima. 'He is a warrior made out of offal!'

Thus admonished, Tŭngku Pănglîma sent about a hundred of his men to kill To' Kâya, but after they had gone some fifty yards they came back to him, and though he bade them go many times, the same thing occurred over and over again.

Suddenly, old Tŭngku Dâlam came hurrying into the palace yard, very much out of breath, for he is of a full habit of body, binding on his *kris* as he ran. 'What is this that men say about To' Kâya running *âmok* in the palace? Where is he?' he cried.

'At the Mosque,' said twenty voices.

'Ya Allah!' said Tŭngku Dâlam, 'They said he was in the palace! Well, what motion are ye making to slay him?'

No one spoke, and Tŭngku Dâlam, cursing them roundly, sent for about forty guns, and, leading the men himself, he passed out at the back of the palace to Tŭngku Chik Pâya's house near the mosque, where To' Kâya still sat upon the low wall which surrounds that building. When he saw Tŭngku Dâlam, he hailed him, saying:

'Welcome! Welcome! Thy servant has desired the long night through to fight with one who is of noble birth. Come, therefore, and let us see which of us twain is the more skilful with his weapons.'

At this, Mat, one of Tŭngku Dâlam's men, leaped forward and said, 'Suffer thy servant to fight with him, it is not fitting, Tŭngku, that thou shouldst take part in such a business.'

But Tŭngku Dâlam said: 'Have patience. He is a dead man. Why should we, who are alive, risk death or hurt at his hands?' Then he ordered a volley to be fired, but when the smoke had cleared away, To' Kâya was still sitting unharmed on the low wall of the mosque. A second volley was fired, with a like result, and then To' Kâya cast away the spear he still held in his hand, and cried out: 'Perchance this spear is a charm against bullets, try once more, and I pray thee end this business, for it has taken over long in the settling.'

A third volley was then fired, and one bullet struck To' Kâya, but did not break the skin. He rubbed the place, and leaped up crying: 'Oh! but that hurts me, I will repay thee!' and, as he rushed at them, the men fell back before him. With difficulty Tŭngku Dâlam succeeded in rallying them, and, this time, a volley was fired, one bullet of which took effect, passing in at one armpit and out at the other. To' Kâya staggered back to the wall, and sank upon it, rocking his body to and fro. Then a final volley rang out, and a bullet passing through his head, he fell forward upon his face. The cowardly crowd surged forward, but fell back again in confusion, for the whisper spread among them that To' Kâya was feigning death in order to get at close quarters. At length a boy named Sâmat, who was related to the deceased Ma' Chik, summoned courage to run in and transfix the body with his spear. Little cared the Dâto' Kâya Bîji Dĕrja, however, for his soul had 'past to where beyond these voices there is peace.'

He had killed his wife, Che' Long, the Kĕlantan man Äbdul Rahman, Pa' Pek, Ma' Pek, Tŭngku Long Pĕndêkar, Ma' Chik, Haji Mih, and Sĕmäil; and had wounded his baby child, his mother-in-law, Che' Long's daughter Ĕsah, and Saleh. This is a sufficiently big butcher's bill for a single man, and he had done all this because he had had words with his wife, and, having gone further than he had intended in the beginning, felt that it would be an unclean thing for him to continue to live upon the surface of a comparatively clean planet. A white man who had stabbed his wife in the heat of the moment might not improbably have committed suicide in his remorse, which would have been far more convenient for his neighbours; but that is one of the many respects in which a white man differs from a Malay.

THE FLIGHT OF CHÊP, THE BIRD

When my foe is in my hands,
When before me pale he stands,
  When he finds no means to fight,
When he knows that death awaits him
At the hands of one who hates him,
  And his looks are wild with fright;
When I stare him in the eyes,
Watch the apple fall and rise
  In the throat his hard sobs tear ;
O, I'll mark his pain with pleasure,
And I'll slay him at my leisure,
  But I'll kill, and will not spare.
        The Song of the Savage Foeman.

IN a large Sâkai camp on the Jĕlai river, at a point some miles above the last of the scattered Malay villages, the annual Harvest Home was being held one autumn night in the Year of Grace 1893. The occasion of the feast was the same as that which all tillers of the soil are wont to celebrate with bucolic rejoicings, and the name, which I have applied to it, calls up in the mind of the exile many a well-loved scene in the quiet country land at Home. Again he sees the loaded farm carts labouring over the grass or rolling down the leafy lanes, again the smell of the hay is in his nostrils, and the soft English gloaming is stealing over the land. The more or less intoxicated reapers astride upon the load exchange their barbarous badinage with those who follow on foot; the pleasant glow of health, that follows upon a long day of hard work in the open air, warms the blood; and in the eyes of all is the light of expectation, born of a memory of the good red meat, and the lashings of sound ale and sour cider, awaiting them at the farmhouse two miles across the meadows.

But in the distant Sâkai country the Harvest Home has little in common with such scenes as these. The *pâdi* planted in the clearing, hard by the spot in which the camp is pitched, has been reaped painfully and laboriously in the native fashion, each ripe ear being severed from its stalk separately and by hand. Then, after many days, the grain has at last been stored in the big bark boxes, under cover of the palm leaf thatch, and the Sâkai women, who have already performed the lion's share of the work, are set to husk some portions of it for the evening meal. This they do with clumsy wooden pestles, held as they stand erect round a sort of trough, the ding-dong-ding of the pounders carrying far and wide through the forest, and, at the sound, all wanderers from the camp turn their faces homeward with the eagerness born of empty stomachs and the prospect of a good meal. The grain is boiled in cooking pots, if the tribe possess any, or, if they are wanting, in the hollow of a bamboo, for that marvellous jungle growth is used for almost every conceivable purpose by natives of the far interior. The fat new rice is sweet to eat. It differs as much from the parched and arid stuff you know in Europe, as does the creamy butter in a cool Devonshire dairy from the liquid yellow train oil which we dignify by that name in the sweltering tropics, and the cooked grain is eaten ravenously, and in incredible quantities by the hungry, squalid creatures in a Sâkai camp. These poor wretches know that, in a day or two, the Malays will come up stream to 'barter' with them, and that the priceless rice will be taken from them, almost by force, in exchange for a few axe-heads and native wood knives. Therefore, the Sâkai eat while there is yet time, and while distended stomachs will still bear the strain of a few additional mouthfuls.

Thus is the harvest home supper devoured in a Sâkai camp, with gluttony and beast noises of satisfaction, while the darkness is falling over the land; but, when the meal has been completed, the sleep of repletion may not fall upon the people. The Spirits of the Woods and of the Streams, and the Demons of the grain must be thanked for their gifts, and propitiated for such evil as has been done them. The forests have been felled to make the clearing, the crop has been reaped, and the rice stored by the tribe. Clearly the Spirits stand in need of comfort for the loss they have sustained, and the Sâkai customs provide for such emergencies. The house of the Chief or the Medicine Man—the largest hut in the camp—is filled to the roof with the sodden green growths of the jungle. The Sâkai have trespassed on the domains of the Spirits, and now the Demons of the Woods are invited to share the dwellings of men. Then, when night has fallen, the Sâkai, men, women, and little children, creep into the house, stark naked and entirely unarmed, and sitting huddled together in the darkness, under the shelter of the leaves and branches with which the place is crammed, raise their voices in a weird chant, which peals skyward till the dawn has come again.

No man can say how ancient is this custom, nor yet the beginnings in which it had its origin. Does it date back to a period when huts and garments, even of bark, were newly acquired things, and when the Sâkai suffered both ungladly after the manner of all wild jungle creatures? Did they, in those days, cast aside their bark loin clothes, and revel once more in pristine nakedness, and in the green things of the forest, on all occasions of rejoicing? We can only speculate, and none can tell us whether we guess aright. But year after year, in a hundred camps throughout the broad Sâkai country, the same ceremony is performed, and the same ancient chant goes up through the still night air, on the day which marks the bringing home of the harvest. The Malays call this practice *bĕr-jĕrmun*, because they trace a not altogether fanciful resemblance between the sheds stuffed with jungle and the *jĕrmun*, or nest-like huts which wild boars construct for their shelter and comfort. But although the Malays, as a race, despise the Sâkai, and all their heathenish ways, on the occasion of which I write, Kria, a man of their nation, was present, and taking an active part in the demon-worship of the Infidels.

What was he doing here, in the remote Sâkai camp, herding naked among the green stuff with the chanting jungle people? He was a Malay of the Malays, a Muhammadan, who, in his sane moments, hated all who prayed to devils, or bowed down to stocks and stones, but, for the moment, he was mad. He had come up stream a few weeks before to barter with the forest dwellers, and the flashing glance from a pair of bright eyes, set in the pale yellow face of a slender Sâkai girl, had blinded him, and bereft him of reason. Life no longer seemed to hold anything of good for him unless Chêp, the Bird, as her people called her, might be his. In the abstract he despised the Sâkai as heartily as ever, but, for the sake of this girl, he smothered his feelings, dwelt among her people as one of themselves, losing thereby the last atom of his self-respect, and finally consented to risk his soul's salvation by joining in their superstitious ceremonies. Yet all this sacrifice had hitherto been unavailing, for Chêp was the wife of a Sâkai named Ku-îsh, or the Porcupine, who guarded her jealously, and gave Kria no opportunity of prosecuting his intimacy with the girl.

On her side, she had quickly divined that Kria had fallen a victim to her charms, and, as he was younger than Ku-îsh, richer, and, moreover, a Malay, a man of a superior race, she was both pleased and flattered. No one who knows what a Sâkai's life is, nor of the purely haphazard manner in which they are allowed to grow up, would dream of looking for principle in a Sâkai woman, or would expect her to resist a temptation. The idea of right and wrong, as we understand it, never probably occurred to Chêp, and all she waited for was a fitting time at which to elope with her Malay lover.

Their chance came on the night of the Harvest Home. In the darkness Kria crept close to Chêp, and, when the chant was at its loudest, he whispered in her ear that his dug-out lay ready by the river bank, and that he loved her. Together they stole out of the hut, unobserved by the Sâkai folk, who sang and grovelled in the darkness. The boat was found, and the lovers, stepping into it, pushed noiselessly out into the stream. The river at this point runs furiously over a sloping bed of shingle, and the roar of its waters soon drowned the splashing of the paddles. Chêp held the steering oar, and Kria, squatting in the bows, propelled the boat with quick strong strokes. Thus they journeyed on in silence, save for an occasional word of endearment from one to the other, until the dawn had broken, and a few hours later they found themselves at the Malay village at which Kria lived. They had come down on a half freshet, and that, in the far upper country, where the streams tear over their pebbly or rocky beds through the gorges formed by the high banks, means travelling at a rushing headlong pace. When the fugitives finally halted at Kria's home, fifty miles separated them from the Sâkai camp, and they felt themselves safe from pursuit.

To understand this, you must realise what the Sâkai of the interior is. Men of his race who have lived for years surrounded by Malay villages are as different from him, as the fallow-deer in an English park from the Sambhur of the jungles. Sâkai who have spent all their lives among Malays, who have learned to wear clothes, and to count up to ten, or may be twenty, are hardly to be distinguished from their neighbours, the other ignorant up country natives. They are not afraid to wander through the villages, they do not rush into the jungle or hide behind trees at the approach of strangers, a water-buffalo does not inspire them with as much terror as a tiger, and they do not hesitate to make, comparatively speaking, long journeys from their homes if occasion requires. In all this they differ widely from the semi-wild Sâkai of the centre of the Peninsula. These men trade with the Malays, it is true, but the trade has to be carried on by visitors who penetrate into the Sâkai country for the purpose. Most of them have learned to speak Malay, though many know only their own primitive language, and when their three numerals, *na-nu*, *nar*, and *nê*—one, two, and three—have been used, fall back for further expression of arithmetical ideas on the word *Kĕrpn*, which means 'many.' For clothes they wear the narrow loin cloth, fashioned from the bark of certain trees, which only partially covers their nakedness; they are as shy as the beasts of the forest, and never willingly do they quit that portion of the country which is still exclusively inhabited by the aboriginal tribes. It was to semi-wild Sâkai such as these that Chêp and her people belonged.

There are tribes of other and more savage jungle-dwellers living in the forests of the broad Sâkai country, men who fly to the jungles even when approached by the tamer tribesmen. Their camps may be seen, on a clear day, far up the hillsides on the jungle-covered uplands of the remote interior; their tracks are occasionally to be met with mixed with those of the bison and the rhinoceros, the deer and the wild swine, but the people themselves are but rarely encountered. The tamer Sâkai trade with them, depositing the articles of barter at certain spots in the forest, whence they are removed by the wild men and replaced by various kinds of jungle produce. Of these, the most valued are the long straight reeds, found only in the most distant fastnesses of the forest, which are used by the tamer tribes to form the inner casing of their blow-pipes.

Chêp had the traditions of her people, and her great love for Kria had alone served to nerve her to leave her tribe, and the forest country that she knew. A great fear fell upon her when, the familiar jungles being left far behind, she found herself floating down stream through cluster after cluster of straggling Malay villages. The knowledge that Kria was at hand to protect her tended to reassure her, but the instinct of her race was strong upon her, and her heart beat violently, like that of some wild bird held in a human hand. All her life the Malays, who preyed upon her people, had been spoken of with fear and terror by the simple Sâkai at night time round the fires in their squalid camps. Now she found herself alone in the very heart—so it seemed to her—of the Malay country. Kria, while he lived among her people as one of themselves, had seemed to her merely a superior kind of Sâkai. Now she realised that he was in truth a Malay, one of the dominant foreign race, and her spirit sank within her. None the less, it never occurred to her to fear pursuit. She knew how much her tribesmen dreaded the Malays, and how strongly averse they were to quitting the forest lands with which they were familiar, and Kria, who had recently acquired a considerable knowledge of the Sâkai ways and customs, felt as confident as she.

So Chêp and her lover halted at the latter's village, and took up their abode in his house. The girl was delighted with her new home, which, in her eyes, seemed a veritable palace, when compared with the miserable dwelling places of her own people; and the number and variety of the cooking pots, and the large stock of household stores filled her woman's soul with delight. Also, Kria was kind to her, and she eat good boiled rice daily, which was a new and a pleasant experience. Sooner or later the importunate longing for the jungle, which is born in the hearts of all forest dwellers, would rise up and drive her back to her own people, but of this she knew nothing, and for the time she was happy.

In the Sâkai camp it was not until day had dawned that the demon-worshippers, looking at one another through heavy sleepless eyes, set in pallid faces, among the draggled greenery in the house, noted that two of their number were missing. The quick sight of the jungle people soon spied the trail of a man and a woman, and, following it, they crowded down to the place where the boat had been moored. Here they squatted on the ground and began to smoke. '*Rĕj-ă-rŏj!*'— 'She is lost!'—they said laconically, in the barbarous jargon of the jungle people, and then relapsed into silence.

'May they be devoured by a tiger!' snarled Ku-îsh, the Porcupine, deep down in his throat, and, at the word, all his hearers shuddered. The curse is the most dreadful that the jungle people know, and if you shared your home with the great cats, as they do, you would regard it with equal fear and respect. Ku-îsh said little more, but he went back to the camp and unslung an exceedingly ancient match-lock, which hung from a beam of the roof in the Chief's hut. It was the only gun in the camp, and was the most precious possession of the tribe, but no man asked him what he was doing, or tried to stay him when he presently plunged into the jungle heading down stream.

Two days later, in the cool of the afternoon, Kria left Chêp in the house busy with the evening's rice, and, accompanied by a small boy, his son by a former marriage, he went to seek for fish in one of the swamps at the back of the village. These marshy places, which are to be found in the neighbourhood of many Malay *Kampongs*, are ready-made rice fields, but since the cultivation of a a *pâdi* swamp requires more exacting labour than most Malays are prepared to bestow upon it, they are often left to lie fallow, while crops are grown in clearings on the neighbouring hills. In dry weather the cracked, parched earth, upon which no vegetation sprouts, alone marks the places which, in the rainy season, are pools of stagnant water, but so sure as there is a pond, there also are the little muddy fish which the Malays call *rûan* and *sĕpat*. Where they vanish to when the water in which they live is licked up by the sunrays, or how they support life during a long season of drought, no man clearly knows, but it is believed that they burrow deep into the earth, and live in the moist mud underfoot until better times come with the heavy tropic rain.

Kria carried two long *jôran*, or native fishing rods, over his shoulder, and his little naked son pattered along at his heels, holding a tin containing bait in his tiny hands. The boy crooned to himself, after the manner of native children, but his father walked along in silence. Arrived at the swamp, which was now a broad pool of water, with here and there a tuft of rank rushes showing above the surface, Kria and his child each took a rod and began patiently angling for the little fish. The sun crept lower and lower down the western sky, till its slanting rays painted the surface of the pool to the crimson hue of blood. The clouds were dyed with a thousand gorgeous tints, and the soft light of the sunset hour mellowed all the land. Kria had seen the same sight many a hundred times before, and he looked on it with the utter indifference to the beauties of nature, which is one of the least attractive characteristics of Malays. If the reddened pool at his feet suggested anything to him, it was only that the day was waning, and that it was time to be wending his way homeward.

He began to gather up his fishing tackle, while his son, squatting on the ground, passed a rattan cord through the fishes' gills to their mouths, so that the take might be carried with greater ease. While they were so engaged, a slight rustle in the high grass behind them caused both father and son to start and look round. Not a breath of wind was blowing, but, none the less, a few feet away from them, the tops of the grass moved slightly, as though the stalks were brushed against by the passage of some wild animal.

'Hasten, little one,' said Kria, uneasily; 'it is a tiger.'

But, as he spoke the words, the grass was parted by human hands, and Kria found himself looking into the wild and angry eyes of Ku-îsh, the Porcupine, along the length of an ancient gun barrel. He had time to note the rust upon the dulled metal, the fantastic shape of the clumsy sight, and the blue tatoo marks on the nose and forehead of his enemy. All these things he saw mechanically, in an instant of time, but before he had moved hand or foot the world seemed to break in fragments around him, to the sound of a furious deafening explosion, and he lay dead upon the sward with his skull shattered to atoms, and the bloody, mucous strings of brain flecking the fresh green grass.

At the sight, Kria's son fled screaming along the edge of the pool, but Ku-îsh's blood was up, and he started in pursuit. The child threw himself down in the long grass, and, raising his little arms above his cowering head, shrieked for mercy in his pure shrill treble voice. Ku-îsh, for answer, plunged his spear again and again through the little writhing body, and, at the second blow, the expression of horror and fear faded from the tender rounded face, and was replaced by that look of perfect rest and peace which is only to be seen in the countenance of a sleeping child.

Ku-îsh gathered up the fish, and took all the tobacco he could find on Kria's body, for a Sâkai rarely loses sight completely of those cravings of appetite, which, with him, are never wholly satisfied. Then, when the darkness had shut down over the land, he crept to Kria's house, and bade Chêp follow him. She came without a word, for women whose ancestors have been slaves for generations have very little will of their own. She wept furtively when Ku-îsh told her, in a few passionless sentences, that he had killed Kria and his son, and she bewailed herself aloud when, at their first halting-place, she received the severe chastisement, which Ku-îsh dealt out to her with no grudging hand, as her share in the general punishment. But, when the thrashing was over, she followed him meekly, with the tears still wet upon her cheeks, making no attempt to escape. Thus Ku-îsh, the Porcupine, and Chêp, the Bird, made their way through the strange forests, until they had once more regained the familiar Sâkai country, and were safe among their own people.

Pursuit into such a place is impossible, for a Sâkai comes and goes like a shadow, and can efface himself utterly when he desires to do so. Thus, though Kria's relatives clamoured for vengeance, little could be done. I was myself at that time in charge of the district in which these things occurred, and it was only by the most solemn promises that no evil should befall them, that I induced the various Sâkai chiefs to meet me near the limits of their country. My request that Ku-îsh should be handed over for trial was received by the assembled elders as a demand which was manifestly ridiculous. Ku-îsh was in the jungle, and they knew that pursuit would be useless, unless his own people aided in the chase. This they were determined not to do, and I, being bound by promises not to harm the Chiefs, was powerless to force them to come to my assistance.

At length, a very aged man, the principal headman present, a wrinkled old savage, scarred by encounters with wild beasts, and mottled with skin disease and dirt, lifted up his voice and spoke, shaking his straggling mop of frowsy grizzled hair in time to the words he uttered.

'There is a custom, *Tûan*, when such things occur. The Porcupine has killed the *Gob* (Malay), and our tribe must repay sevenfold. Seven lives for a life. It is the custom.'

The proposal sounded generous, and I was inclined to jump at it, until, on inquiry, I discovered what the ancient chief really intended. His suggestion was that the blood-money should take the form of seven human beings, who were to be duly delivered to the relations of the murdered man as slaves. These seven creatures were not to be members of his or Ku-îsh's tribe, but were to be captured by them from among the really wild people of the hills, who had had no share in the ill-doing which it was my object to punish. The Porcupine and his brethren, he explained, would run some risk, and be put to a considerable amount of trouble, before the seven wild men could be caught, and this was to be the measure of their punishment. The old Chief went on to tell me that the wild Sâkai only pursued a raiding party until they came to a spot where a spear had been left sticking upright in the ground. This custom, he said, was well known to the marauders, who took care to avail themselves of it, so soon as their captives had been secured. My informant said that the wild men would never venture past a spear left in this manner, but he was unable to explain the reason, and did not profess to understand the superstition with which this spear is probably connected in the minds of the jungle dwellers.

Blood-money in past times, I was assured both by Malays and Sâkai, had always been paid in this manner by the semi-wild tribes of the interior. It was the custom, and Kria's relatives were eager in their prayers to me to accept the proposal. Instead, I exacted a heavy fine of jungle produce from the tribe to which Ku-îsh, the Porcupine, belonged, and thus I gave complete dissatisfaction to all parties concerned. The Sâkai disliked the decision because they found the fine more difficult to pay, while the Malays thought the blood-money paid hopelessly inadequate, when compared with the value of seven slaves. But, as the Indian Proverb says, 'an order is an order until one is strong enough to disobey it.' Therefore the fine was paid by the Sâkai and accepted by the Malays with grumblings, of which I only heard the echoes.

So ends the story of the Flight of Chêp, the Bird, and of the deed whereby Ku-îsh, the Porcupine, cleansed his honour from the shame that had been put upon him. The murder was a brutal act, savagely done, and the ruthless manner in which the Porcupine killed the little defenceless child, who had done no evil to him or his, makes one's blood boil. None the less, when one remembers the heavy debt of vengeance, for long years of grinding cruelty and wicked wrong, which the Sâkai owes to the Malay, one can find it in one's heart to forgive much that he may do when the savage lust of blood is upon him, and when, for a space, his enemies of the hated race are delivered into his hand.

THE VAULTING AMBITION

> Adown the stream, whence mist like steam
>   Arises in early morning,
> 'Mid shout and singing they bear me swinging
>   A mark for the people's scorning.
> By long hair hanging, amid the clanging
>   Of drums that are beaten loud,
> I am borne—the Head of the ghastly Dead,
>   That ne'er knew coffin nor shroud !
> But I swing there, nor greatly care
>   If the Victor jeers or sings,
> Nor heed my foe, for now I know
>   The worth of these mortal things.
>   *The Song of the Severed Head.*

WHEN the Portuguese Filibusters descended upon the Peninsula, they employed—so says the native tradition—the time-worn stratagem of the Pious Æneas ; and, having obtained, by purchase, as much land as could be enclosed by the hide of a bull, from the Sultân of Malacca, they cut the skin up into such cunning strips that a space large enough to build a formidable fort was won by them. This they erected in the very heart of the capital, which, at that time, was the head and front of the Malay Kingdoms of the Peninsula. Thence they speedily overran the State of Malacca, and, though the secret of making gunpowder, and rude match-locks, was known to the Malays, native skill and valour was of no avail when opposed to the discipline and the bravery of the mail-clad Europeans. Thus, the country was soon subdued, and, in 1511, Sultân Muhammad, with most of his relations and a few faithful followers, fled to Pahang, which, at that time, was a dependency of Malacca. Here he founded a new Dynasty, his descendants assuming the title of Bĕndăhâra, and doing homage and owing allegiance to the Sultân of Daik, whose kingdom, in its turn, has since fallen to the portion of the Dutch.

The people of Pahang were ever lawless, warlike folk, and the Malacca *Râjas*, who seem to have been a mild enough set of people while in their own country, speedily caught the infection from their surroundings. Thus, from one generation to another, various rival claimants to the throne strove for the mastery during successive centuries. The land was always more or less on the rack of civil war, and so to-day the largest State in the Peninsula carries a population of only some four human beings to the square mile.

War was lulled, and peace fell upon Pahang when Bĕndahâra Äli, the father of the present Sultân, came to the throne ; but, when he died in his palace among the cocoa-nut trees, across the river opposite to the Pĕkan of to-day, civil war broke out once more with redoubled fury. During the years that he was a fugitive from the land of his birth, Che' Wan Âhmad, who now bears the high-sounding title of Sultân Âhmad Maätham, Shah of Pahang, made numerous efforts to seize the throne from his brother and nephew, but it was not until the fifth attempt that he was finally successful.

During one of those pauses which occurred in the war game, when Âhmad had once more been driven into exile, and his brother's son Bĕndăhâra Korish reigned in Pahang, the ambitions of Wan Bong of Jĕlai brought him who had cherished them to an untimely and ignoble death.

The Jĕlai valley has, from time immemorial, been ruled over by a race of Chiefs, who, though they are regarded by the other natives of Pahang as ranking merely as nobles, are treated by the people of their own district with semi-royal honours. The Chief of the Clan, the Dâto' Mahrâja Pĕrba Jĕlai, commonly known as To' Râja, is addressed as *Ungku*, which means 'Your Highness,' by his own people. Homage too is done to him by them, hands being lifted up in salutation, with the palms pressed together, as in the attitude of Christian prayer, but the tips of the thumbs are not suffered to ascend beyond the base of the chin. In saluting a real *Râja*, the hands are carried higher and higher, according to the prince's rank, until, for the Sultân, the tips of the thumbs are on a level with the forehead. Little details, such as these, are of immense importance in the eyes of the Malays, and not without reason, seeing that, in an Independent Native State, many a man has come by his death for carelessness in their observance. A wrongly given salute may raise the ire of a *Râja*, which is no pleasant thing to encounter; or if it flatter him by giving him more than his due, the fact may be whispered in the ears of his superiors, who will not be slow to resent the usurpation and to punish the delinquent.

At the time of which I write, the then To' Râja of Jĕlai was an aged man, cursed by the possession of many sons, arrogant folk, who loved war. The eldest, the most arrogant, the most warlike, the most ambitious, and the most evil of these, was Wan Bong. He, the people of the Jĕlai called Che' Âki, which means 'Sir Father,' because he was the heir of their Dàto', or Chief, which word in the vernacular literally means a grandfather. He was a man of about thirty-five years of age, of a handsome presence, and an aristocratic bearing. He wore his fine black hair long, so that it hung about his waist, and he dressed with the profusion of coloured silks, and went armed with the priceless weapons, that are only to be seen in perfection on the person of a Malay prince. Into the mind of this man there entered, on a certain day, an idea at once daring and original. Ever since the death of Bĕndâhâra Äli, nearly a decade earlier, Pahang had been racked by war and rumours of war, and, wherever men congregated, tales were told of the brave deeds done by the rival *Râjas*, each of whom was seeking to win the throne for himself and for his posterity. It was the memory of these things that probably suggested his project to Wan Bong. Che' Wan Âhmad had fled the country after his last defeat, and Bĕndâhâre Korish, with his sons Che' Wan Âhman, and Che' Wan Da, ruled at Pĕkan. To none of the latter did Wan Bong cherish any feeling but hatred, and it occurred to him that now, while they were still suffering from the effects of their fierce struggle with Che' Wan Âhmad, it would be possible, by a bold stroke, to upset their dynasty, and to secure the broad valleys of Pahang as an inheritance for his father, To' Râja, for himself, and for their heirs for ever.

Every man in Pahang was, at that time, a soldier; and the people of Jĕlai and Lĭpis were among the most warlike of the inhabitants of the country. All the people of the interior followed Wan Bong like sheep, and he speedily found himself at the head of a following of many thousands of men. For a noble to rise up against his sovereign, with the object of placing his own family upon the throne, was an altogether unheard of thing among the natives of the Peninsula; but the very originality of Wan Bong's plan served to impress the people with the probability of its success. The *Râjas* at Pĕkan were very far away, while Wan Bong, with unlimited power in his hands, was at their very doors. Therefore the natives of the upper country had no hesitation in selecting the side to which it was most politic for them to adhere.

Wan Bong installed his father as Bĕndăhâra of Pahang with much state, and many ceremonial observances. All the insignia of royalty were hastily fashioned by the goldsmiths of Pĕnjum, and, whenever To' Râja or Wan Bong appeared in public, they were accompanied by pages bearing betel boxes, swords, and silken umbrellas, as is the manner of Malay kings.

To' Râja remained in his village of Bûkit Bĕtong, on the banks of the Jĕlai river, and Wan Bong, with his army, speedily conquered the whole of Pahang as far as Kuâla Sĕmantan. Thus more than half the country was his, almost without a struggle; and Wan Bong, flustered with victory, returned up river to receive the congratulations of his friends, leaving Pănglîma Râja Sĕbîdi, his principal General, in charge of the conquered districts.

The *Râjas* at Pĕkan, however, were meanwhile mustering their men, and, when Wan Bong reached Kuâla Tĕmbĕling, he received the unwelcome intelligence that his forces had fallen back some sixty miles to Tanjong Gâtal, before an army under the command of Che' Wan Âhman and Che' Wan Da. At Tanjong Gâtal a battle was fought, and the royal forces were routed with great slaughter, as casualties are reckoned in Malay warfare, nearly a score of men being killed. But Che' Wan Âhman knew that many Pahang battles had been won without the aid of gunpowder or bullets, or even *kris* and spear. He sent secretly to Pănglîma Râja Sïbîdi, and, by promises of favours to come, and by gifts of no small value, he had but little difficulty in persuading him to turn traitor. The Pănglîma was engaged in a war against the ruler of the country, the Khalîfah, the earthly representative of the Prophet on Pahang soil, and the feeling that he was thus warring against God, as well as against man, probably made him the more ready to enrich himself by making peace with the princes to whom he rightly owed allegiance. Be this how it may, certain it is that Pănglîma Râja Sĕbîdi went to Wan Bong, where he lay camped at Kuâla Tĕmbĕling, and assured him that after the defeat at

Tanjong Gâtal, the royal forces had dispersed, and that the Pĕkan *Rájas* were now in full flight.

'Pahang is now thine, O Prince!' he concluded, 'so be pleased to return to the Jĕlai, and I, thy servant, will keep watch and ward over the conquered land, until such time as thou bringest thy father with thee, to sit upon the throne which thy valour has won for him, and for his seed for ever!'

So Wan Bong set off on a triumphal progress up river to Bûkit Bĕtong, disbanding his army as he went. But scarcely had he reached his home, than he learned, to his dismay, that Che' Wan Âhman and Che' Wan Da, with a large force, were only a few miles behind him at Bâtu Nĕring. Pănglîma Râja Sĭbîdi, with all his people, had made common cause with the enemy, whose ranks were further swelled by the very men who had so lately been disbanded by Wan Bong on his journey up river. The Pĕkan *Rájas* had carefully collected them man by man as they followed in the wake of the dispersing army, and Wan Bong thus found himself deprived, in an instant, not only of all that he had believed himself to have won, but even of such poor following as had been his in the days before his ambitious schemes were hatched.

But before the royal forces began their invasion of the upper country, it became evident to them that Che' Jahya, the Chief who had been left in charge of the Tĕmbĕling River by Wan Bong, must be disposed of. This man had followed Wan Bong's fortunes from the first, and it was known in the royal camp that no attempt to buy his loyalty would be likely to prove successful. Wan Bong had started up the Jĕlai on his triumphal progress, and it was important that no news should reach him, that might cause him to stay the dispersal of his men. So Che' Jahya's fate was sealed. About the second day after Wan Bong's departure for Bûkit Bĕtong, Che' Jahya was seated in the cool interior of his house at Kuâla Âtok, on the Tĕmbĕling River. The sun was hot overhead, and the squeaking low of a cow-buffalo, calling to its calf, came to his ears. The fowls clucked and scratched about the ground beneath the flooring, and the women-folk in the cook-house chattered happily. All spoke of peace. The war was over, and Che' Jahya sat dreaming of the good things which would be his in the days that were coming. He had stood by Wan Bong when bullets were flying, and had camped on the bare earth when his armies had taken the field. His aid and his counsel had had no small share in his chief's success. Che' Jahya's heart was filled with peace, and the gladness of one whose toils are over, and who sees his rewards well within his grasp. Already, in imagination, he was acting as the new Bĕndâhâras deputy, having power over men, a harem full of fair women, and wealth to gild his ease. And yet, as he sat there dreaming, his death was ever drawing nearer to him, unfeared and unsuspected.

Shortly before sunset, at the hour when the kine go down to water, a party of Râwa men came to Che' Jahya's house. These people are a race of Sumatran Malays, and members of their tribe have been mercenaries and hired bravos in the Peninsula, beyond the memory of man. They came to Che' Jahya, they said, to offer their services to him; and, in their coming, he saw the first evidence of that authority over men and things, of which he had sat dreaming through the hot hours of the day. He received them courteously, and had rice and spiced viands placed before them, inviting them to eat, and, in doing so, he almost unconsciously assumed the tone and manners of a great chief. All partook of the meal in heartiness and good fellowship, for the Râwa people have no fine feelings about abusing hospitality, and a meal, come by it how you may, is a meal, and as such is welcome. When the food had been disposed of, and quids of betel nut and cigarettes were being discussed, the talk naturally turned upon the war, which had so recently closed. Che' Jahya, still living in his Fool's Paradise, and intoxicated by his new honours and importance, was blind to any suspicions of treachery, which, at another time, might have presented themselves to him. He spoke condescendingly to his guests, still aping the manners of a great chief. He dropped a passing hint or two of his own prowess in the war, and when Băginda Sutan, the Headman of the Râwa gang, craved leave to examine the beauties of his *kris*, he handed his weapon to him, without hesitation, and with the air of one who confers a favour upon his subordinate.

This was the psychological moment for which his guests had been waiting. So long as Che' Jahya was armed, it was possible that he might be able to do one of them a hurt, which was opposed to the principles upon which the Râwa men were accustomed to work; but as soon as he had parted with his *kris*, all the necessary conditions had been complied with. At a sign from their Chief, three of the Râwa men snatched up their guns, and a moment later Che' Jahya rolled over dead, with three gaping holes drilled through his body. There he lay, motionless, in an ever-widening pool of blood, on the very spot where, so few hours before, he had dreamed those dreams of power and greatness—dreams that had then soared so high, and now lay as low as he, crushed and obliterated from the living world, as though they had never been.

Sutan Băginda hacked off Che' Jahya's head, salted it, for obvious reasons, stained it a ghastly yellow with turmeric, as a further act of dishonour, and, when the house and village had been looted, carried his ghastly trophy with him down river to the camp of Che' Wan Âhman. Then it was fastened to a boat pole, fixed upright in the sand of Pâsir Tambang, at the mouth of the Těmběling River, where it dangled with all the horror of set teeth, and staring eyeballs—the fixity of the face of one who has died a violent death—until, in the fulness of time, the waters rose and swept pole and head away with them. Thus was a plain lesson taught, by Che' Wan Âhman to the people of Pahang, as a warning to dreamers of dreams.

But to return to Wan Bong, whose high hopes had all been shattered as completely, and almost as rudely, as those of poor Che' Jahya. When the evil news of the approach of Che' Wan Âhman and his people reached him, Wan Bong's scant following dwindled rapidly, and, at length, he was forced to seek refuge in the jungles of the Jělai, with only three or four of his closest adherents still following his fallen fortunes. As he lay on his bed of boughs, under a hastily improvised shelter of plaited palm leaves, with the fear of imminent death staring him in the eyes; when through the long day every snapping twig and every falling fruit, in those still forests, must have sounded to his ears like the footfall of his pursuers, Wan Bong must have had ample time to contrast his past position with that in which he then found himself. A few days before, he had returned to Jĕlai, a conqueror flushed with triumph. All Pahang, he had then imagined, lay at his feet, and he alone, of all the nobles of the Peninsula, had in a few months upset an old-world dynasty, and placed himself upon a royal throne. Then, in an instant of time, the vision had been shattered to fragments, and here he lay, like a hunted beast in the jungles, quaking at every sound that broke the stillness, an outlaw, a ruined man, with a price set upon his head.

The jungles, for a fugitive from his enemies, are not a pleasant refuge. The constant dampness, which clings to anything in the dark recesses of the forest, breeds boils and skin irritation of all sorts on the bodies of those who dare not come out into the open places. Faces, on which the sunlight never falls, become strangely pallid, and the constant agony of mind scores deep lines on cheek and forehead. The food, too, is bad. Rice the fugitive must have, or the loathsome dropsical swellings, called *bâsal*, soon cripple the strongest limbs; but a Malay cannot live on rice alone, and the sour jungle fruits, and other vegetable growths, with which he ekes out his scanty meals, wring his weakened stomach with constant pangs and aches. All these things Wan Bong now experienced, as he daily shifted his camp, from one miserable halting-place to another; but a greater pain than all the rest was soon to be added to his cup of bitterness. He was an opium smoker, and his hoarded store of the precious drug began to run very low. At last the day came on which it was exhausted, and Wan Bong was driven to desperation. For some twenty-four hours he strove against the overpowering longing for that subtle drug that leads the strongest will captive, but the struggle was all in vain. When, at length, the physical pain had become so intense that Wan Bong could neither stand, nor sit, nor lie down for more than a minute at a time, nor yet could still the moans which the restless torture drew from him, he despatched one of his boys to seek for the supply of opium, which alone could assuage his sufferings.

The boy left him, and his two other companions, in a patch of the high grass, which the Malays call *rĕsam*, that chanced to grow at the edge of the forest near Bâtu Nĕring. He promised to return to him as soon as the opium should have been procured. But Che' Wan Âhman's people had anticipated that Wan Bong would, sooner or later, be forced to purchase opium, and no sooner had the messenger presented himself at the shop of the Chinese trader, who sold the drug, than he found himself bound hand and foot. He was carried before Che' Wan Âhman's representative, and interrogated. He denied all knowledge of Wan Bong's hiding-place; but Malays have methods of making people speak the truth on occasion. They are grim, ghastly, blood-curdling methods, that need not be here described in detail; suffice it to say that the boy spoke.

That evening, as the short twilight was going out in the sky, and the flakes of scarlet-dyed clouds were paling overhead, a body of men crept, with noiseless feet, through the clump of long grass in which Wan Bong was hiding. They saw him sitting on the earth, bent double over his folded arms, rocking his body to and fro, in the agony of the opium smoker, when the unsatisfied craving for the drug is strong upon him. There was a rustle in the grass behind him, the sharp fierce clang of a rifle rang out through the forest, and a bullet through Wan Bong's back ended his pains for ever. The Headman of the pursuing band was Che' Bûrok of Pûlau Tâwar, but he was a prudent person who kept well in the rear until the deed had been done. Then he came forward rapidly, and unstringing the purse-belt from around his waist, he gave it to the man who had fired the shot, in exchange for a promise that not he, but Che' Bûrok, should have the credit which is due to one who has slain the enemies of the King. Thus it was that Che' Bûrok was credited, for a time, with the deed, and reaped fair rewards from the Bĕndăhâra and his sons. But murder will out, and Che' Bûrok died some years later, a discredited liar, in disgrace with his former masters, and shorn of all his honours and possessions.

Wan Bong's head was sawn off at the neck, and was carried into camp, by that splendid shock of luxuriant black hair, which had been his pride when he was alive. It was clotted with blood now, and matted with the dirt from the lairs where he had slept in the jungle, but it served well enough as a handle by which to hold his dissevered head, and there was no need, therefore, to make a puncture under his chin, whence to pass a rattan cord through to his mouth, as is the custom when there is no natural handle by which such trophies can be carried.

On Che' Bûrok's arrival in camp, the head was salted, as Che' Jahya's had been, and, like his, it was also smeared with turmeric. Then, when the dawn had broken, it was fastened, still by its luxuriant hair, to the horizontal bar which supports the forward portion of the punting platform on a Malay boat, and the *prâhu,* with its ghastly burden, started down river to Pĕkan, to the sound of beating drums, and clanging gongs, and to the joyous shouts of the men at the paddles. For two hundred odd miles they bore this present to their King, down all the glorious reaches of river, glistening in the sunlight, that wind through the length of the Pahang valley. The people of the villages came out upon the river banks, and watched the procession file past them with silent, unmoved countenances, and all the long way the distorted head of him, whose eyes had looked with longing on a throne, shook gently from side to side, with the motion of the boat, as though he still was musing sadly on the schemes which had brought him to his bloody death.

'ONE MORE UNFORTUNATE'

> For the gods very subtly fashion
> Madness with sadness upon earth :
> Not knowing in any wise compassion,
> Nor holding pity of any worth.
> *Atalanta in Calydon.*

In writing of the *âmok*, which Dâto' Kâya Bîji Dĕrja ran in the streets of Kuâla Trĕnggânu, I have spoken of suicide as being of very rare occurrence among Malays of either sex, and, indeed, I know of no authenticated case in which a man of these people has taken his life with his own hand. A Chinaman, who has had a difference of opinion with a friend, or who conceives that he has been ill-treated by the Powers that be, betakes himself to his dwelling, and there deliberately hangs himself with his pig-tail, dying happy in the pleasing belief that his spirit will haunt those who have done him a wrong, and render the remainder of their lives upon earth 'one demned horrid grind.' Not so the Malay. He, being gifted with the merest rudiments of an imagination, prefers to take practical vengeance on his kind by means of a knife, to trusting to such supernatural retaliation as may be effected after death by his ghost.

This story deals with a suicide which occurred in Pahang in July 1893, and I have selected it to tell, because the circumstances were remarkable, and are quite unprecedented in my experience.

If you go up the Pahang River for a hundred and eighty miles, you come to a spot where the stream divides into two main branches, and where the name Pahang dies an ignominious death in a small ditch, which debouches at their point of junction. The right stream,—using the term in its topographical sense,—is the Jĕlai, and the left is the Tĕmbĕling. If you go up the latter, you come to rapids innumerable, a few *gambir* plantations, and a great many of the best ruffians in the Peninsula, who are also my very good friends. If you follow the Jĕlai up past Kuâla Līpis, where the river of the latter name falls into it on its right bank, and on, and on, and on, you come to the Sâkai country, where the Malay language is still unknown, and where the horizon of the people is formed by the impenetrable jungle that shuts down on the other side of a slender stream, and is further narrowed by the limitations of an intellect which cannot conceive an arithmetical idea higher than the numeral three. Before you run your nose into these uncleanly places, however, you pass through a district dotted with scattered Malay habitations ; and, if you turn off up the Tĕlang River, you find a little open country, and some prosperous-looking villages.

One day in July 1893, a feast in honour of a wedding was being held in one of these places, and the scene was a lively one. The head and skin of a buffalo, and the pools of blood, which showed where its carcase had been dismembered, were a prominent feature in the foreground, lying displayed in a very unappetising manner on a little piece of open ground. In one part of the village two men were posturing in one of the inane sword-dances which are so dear to all Malays, each performance being a subject of keen criticism or hearty admiration to the spectators. The drums and gongs meanwhile beat a rhythmical time, which makes the heaviest heels long to move more quickly, and the onlookers whooped and yelled again and again in shrill far-sounding chorus. The shout is the same as that which is raised by Malays when in battle; and, partly from its tone, and partly from association, one never hears it without a thrill, and some sympathetic excitement. It has a similar effect upon the Malays, who love to raise a *sôrak*,—as these choric shouts are termed,—and the enthusiasm which it arouses is felt to be infectious, and speedily becomes maddening and intense.

All the men present were dressed in many-coloured silks and tartans, and were armed with daggers as befits warriors, but, if you had an eye for such things, you would have noticed that all the garments and weapons were worn in a manner which would have excited the ridicule of a down-country Malay. It is not in Europe only, that the country cousin furnishes food for laughter to his relatives in the towns.

In a *Bâlai*, specially erected for the purposes of the feast, a number of priests, and pilgrims, and *lêbai*,— that class of fictitious religious mendicants, whose members are usually some of the richest men in the villages they inhabit,—were seated gravely intoning the *Kurân*, but stopping to chew betel-nut, and to gossip scandalously, at frequent intervals. The wag, too, was present among them, for he is an inevitable feature in all Malay gatherings, and he is generally one of the local holy men. 'It ain't precisely what 'e says, it's the *funny* way 'e says it;'—for, like the professionally comic man all the world over, these individuals are popularly supposed to be invariably amusing, and a loud guffaw goes up whenever they open their mouths, no matter what the words that issue from them. Most of his hearers had heard his threadbare old jokes any time these twenty years, but the ready laughter greeted each of them in turn, as though they were newly born into the world. A Malay does not understand that a joke may pall from repetition, and is otherwise liable to be driven into the ground. He will ask for the same story, or the same jest time after time; prefers that it should be told in the same manner, and in the same words; and will laugh in the same place, with equal zest, at each repetition, just as do little children among ourselves. A similar failure to appreciate the eternal fitness of things, causes a Malay *Râja*, when civilised, to hang seven copies of the same unlovely photograph around the walls of his sitting-room.

Meanwhile, the women-folk had come from far and near, to help to prepare the feast, and the men, having previously done the heavy work of carrying the water, hewing the firewood, jointing the meat, and crushing the curry stuff, they were all busily engaged in the back premises of the house, cooking as only Malay women can cook, and keeping up a constant babble of shrill trebles, varied by an occasional excited scream of direction from one of the more senior women among them. The younger and prettier girls had carried their work to the door of the house, and thence were engaging at long range in the game of 'eye play,'—as the Malays call it,—with the youths of the village, little heeding the havoc they were making in susceptible male breasts, whose wounds, however, they would be ready enough to heal, as occasion offered, with a limitless generosity.

The bride, of course, having being dressed in her best, and loaded with gold ornaments, borrowed from many miles around, which had served to deck every bride in the district ever since any one could remember, was left seated on the *gĕta*, or raised sleeping platform, in the dimly lighted inner apartments, there to await the ordeal known to Malay cruelty as *sanding*. The ceremony that bears this name, is the one at which the bride and bridegroom are brought together for the first time. They are officially supposed never to have seen one another before, though no Malay who respects himself ever allows his *fiancée* to be finally selected, until he has crept under her house, in the night time, and watched her through the bamboo flooring, or through the chinks in the wattled walls. They are led forth by their respective relations, and placed side by side upon a dais, prepared for the purpose, where they remain seated for hours, while the guests eat a feast in their presence, and thereafter chant verses from the *Kurân*. During this ordeal they must sit motionless, no matter how their cramped legs may ache and throb, and their eyes must remain downcast, and fixed upon their hands, which, scarlet with henna, lie motionless one on each knee. Malays, who have experienced this, tell me that it is very trying, and I can well believe it, the more so, since it is a point of honour for the man to try to catch an occasional glimpse of his *fiancée*, out of the corner of his eyes, without turning his head a hair's breadth, and without appearing to move an eyelash. The bridegroom is conducted to the house of his bride, there to sit in state, by a band of his relations and friends, some of whom sing shrill verses from the *Kurân*, while others rush madly ahead, charging, retreating, capering, dancing, yelling, and hooting, brandishing naked weapons, and engaging in a most realistic sham fight, with the bride's relations and friends, who rush out of her compound to meet them, and do not suffer themselves to be routed until they have made a fine show of resistance. This custom, doubtless, has its origin in the fact that, in primitive states of society, a man must seek a wife at his risk and peril, for among the *Sâkai* in some of the wilder parts of the country, the girl is still placed upon an anthill, and ringed about by her relations, who do not suffer her *fiancé* to win her until his head has been broken in several places. The same *feeling* exists in Europe, as is witnessed by the antagonism displayed by the school-boy, and even the older and more sensible males of a family, to their would-be brother-in-law. It is the natural instinct of the man, to protect his women-folk from all comers, breaking out, as natural instincts are wont to do, in a hopelessly wrong place.

As I have said, the bride had been left in the inner

apartments, there to await her call to the dais ; and the preparations for the feast were in full swing, and the men were enjoying themselves in their own way while the women cooked, when, suddenly, a dull thud, as of some falling body, was heard within the house. The women rushed in, and found the little bride lying on the floor, with all the pretty garments, with which she had been bedecked, drenched in her own blood. A small clasp knife lay by her side, and there was a ghastly gash in her throat. The women lifted her up, and strove to staunch the bleeding, and as they fought to stay the life that was ebbing from her, the drone of the priests, and the beat of the drums, came to their ears from the men who were making merry without. Then suddenly the news of what had occurred spread among the guests, and the music died away, and was replaced by a babble of excited voices, all speaking at once.

The father of the girl rushed in, and, as she lay on the sleeping platform, still conscious, he asked her who had done this thing.

'It is my own handiwork,' she said.

'But wherefore, child of mine,' cried her mother, 'but wherefore dost thou desire to slay thyself?'

'I gazed upon my likeness in the mirror,' said the girl, speaking slowly and with difficulty, 'and I beheld that I was very hideous to look upon, so that it was not fitting that I should live. Therefore I did it.'

And until she died, about an hour later, this, and this only, was the explanation which she would give. The matter was related to me by the great up-country Chief, the Dáto' Mahrâja Pĕrba, who said that he had never heard of any parallel case. I jestingly told him that he should be careful not to allow this deed to become a precedent, for there are many ugly women in his district, and if they all followed this girl's example, the population would soon have dwindled sadly. Later, when I learned the real reasons which led to this suicide, I was sorry that I had ever jested about it, for the girl's was a sad little story.

Some months before, a Pĕkan born Malay had come to the Jĕlai on a trading expedition, and had cast his eyes upon the girl. To her, he was all that the people of the surrounding villages were not. He walked with a swagger, wore his weapons and his clothes with an air that none but a Court-bred Malay knows how to assume, and was full of brave tales, which the elders of the village could only listen to with wonder and respect. As the brilliant form of Lancelot burst upon the startled sight of the Lady of Shalott, so did this man—an equally splendid vision in the eyes of this poor little up-country maid—come into her life, bringing with him hopes and desires, that she had never before dreamed of. Before so brave a wooer what could her little arts avail? As many better and worse women than she have done before her, she gave herself to him, thinking, thereby, to hold him in silken bonds, through which he might not break; but what was all her life to her, was merely a passing incident to him, and one day she learned that he had returned down stream. The idea of following him probably never even occurred to her, but, like others before her, she thought that the sun had fallen from heaven, because her night light had gone out. Her parents, who knew nothing of this intrigue, calmly set about making the arrangements for her marriage, a matter in which, of course, she would be the last person to be consulted. She must have watched these preparations with speechless agony, knowing that the day fixed for the marriage must be that on which her life would end, for she must long have resolved to die faithful to her false lover, though it was not until the very last moment that she summoned up sufficient courage to take her own life. That she ever did so is very marvellous. That act is one which is not only contrary to all natural instincts, but is, moreover, utterly opposed to the ideas which prevail among people of her race; and her sufferings must, indeed, have been intense, before this means of escape can have presented itself to her, even as a possibility. She must have been at once a girl of extraordinary strength and weakness: strength to have made the resolve, and, having made it, to fearlessly carry it into execution, dying with a lie on her lips, which should conceal her real reasons, and the fact of her rapidly approaching maternity; and weakness in that the burden laid upon her was greater than she could bear. Poor child, ignorant, yet filled with a terrible knowledge, false, yet faithful even unto death, strong in her weakness, with a marvellous strength, yet weak in her first fall.

> She has lived her life, and that which she has done,
> May God within Himself make whole.

AMONG THE FISHER FOLK

> A palm-leaf sail that stretches wide,
>   A sea that's running strong,
> A boat that dips its laving side,
>   The forefoot's rippling song.
> A flaming sky, a crimson flood,
>   Here's joy for body and mind,
> As in our canting crafts we scud
>   With a spanking breeze behind.
>
> *The Song of the Fisher Folk.*

THIS is a land of a thousand beauties. Nature, as we see her in the material things which delight our eyes, is straight from the hand of God, unmarred by man's deforming, a marvellous creation of green growths and brilliant shades of colour, fresh, sweet, pure, an endless panorama of loveliness. But it is not only the material things which form the chief beauties of the land in which we dwell. The ever-varying lights of the Peninsula, and the splendid Malayan sky that arches over us are, in themselves, at once the crown of our glory, and the imparters of a fresh and changeful loveliness to the splendours of the earth. Our eyes are ever glutted with the wonders of the sky, and of the lights which are shed around us. From the moment when the dawn begins to paint its orange tints in the dim East, and later floods the vastness of the low-lying clouds with glorious dyes of purple and vermillion, and a hundred shades of colour, for which we have no name, reaching to the very summit of the heavens; on through the early morning hours, when the slanting rays of the sun throw long broad streaks of dazzlingly white light upon the waters of sea and river; on through the burning noonday, when the shadows fall black and sharp and circular, in dwarfed patches about our feet; on through the cooler hours of the afternoon, when the sun is a burning disc low down in the western sky, or, hiding behind a bank of clouds, throws wide-stretched arms of prismatic colour high up into the heavens; on through the hour of sunset, when all the world is a flaming blaze of gold and crimson; and so into the cool still night, when the moon floods us with a sea of light only one degree less dazzling than that of day, or when the thousand wonders of the southern stars gaze fixedly upon us from their places in the deep clear vault above our heads, and Venus casts a shadow on the grass; from dawn to dewy eve, from dewy eve to dawn, the lights of the Peninsula vary as we watch them steep us and all the world in glory, and half intoxicate us with their beauty.

But the sea is the best point or vantage from which to watch the glories of which I tell—speaking as I do in weak colourless words of sights and scenes which no human brush could ever hope to render, nor mortal poet dream of painting in immortal song—and if you would see them for yourself, and drink in their beauty to the full, go dwell among the Fisher Folk of the East Coast.

They are a rough, hard-bit gang, ignorant and superstitious beyond belief, tanned to the colour of mahogany by exposure to the sun, with faces scarred and lined by rough weather and hard winds. They are plucky and reckless, as befits men who go down to the sea in ships; they are full of resource, the results of long experience of danger, and constant practice in sudden emergencies, where a loss of presence of mind means a forfeiture of life. Their ways and all their dealings are bound fast by a hundred immutable customs, handed down through countless ages, which no man among them dreams of violating; and they have, moreover, that measure of romance attaching to them which clings to all men who run great risks, and habitually carry their lives in their hands.

From the beginning of November to the end of February the North-East monsoon whips down the long expanse of the China Sea, fenced as it is by the Philippines and Borneo on the one hand, and by Cochin China and Cambodia on the other, until it breaks in all its force and fury on the East Coast of the Peninsula. It raises breakers mountain high upon the bars at the river mouths, it dashes huge waves against the shore, or banks up the flooded streams as they flow seaward, until, on a calm day, a man may drink sweet water a mile out at sea. During this season the people of the coast are mostly idle, though they risk their lives and their boats upon the fishing banks on days when a treacherous calm lures them seaward, and they can rarely be induced to own that the monsoon has in truth broken, until the beaches have been strewn with driftwood from a dozen wrecks. They long for the open main when they are not upon it, and I have seen a party of Kĕlantan fishermen half drunk with joy at finding themselves dancing through a stormy sea in an unseaworthy craft on a dirty night, after a long period spent on the firm shore. 'It is indeed sweet,' they kept exclaiming—'it is indeed sweet thus once more to play with the waves!' For here as elsewhere the sea has its own peculiar strange fascination for those who are at once its masters, its slaves, and its prey.

When they have at last been fairly beaten by the monsoon, the fisher folk betake themselves to the scattered coast villages, which serve to break the monotonous line of jungle and shivering *casuarina* trees that fringe the sandy beach and the rocky headlands of the shore. Here under the cocoa-nut palms, amid chips from boats that are being repaired, and others that still lie upon the stocks, surrounded by nets, and sails, and masts, and empty crafts lying high and dry upon the beach out of reach of the tide, the fishermen spend the months of their captivity. Their women live here all the year round, labouring incessantly in drying and salting the fish which have been taken by the men, or pounding prawns into *blâchan*, that evil-smelling condiment which has been so ludicrously misnamed the Malayan Caviare. It needs all the violence of the fresh, strong, monsoon winds to even partially purge these villages of the rank odours which cling to them at the end of the fishing season; and when all has been done, the saltness of the sea air, the brackish water of the wells, and the faint stale smells emitted by the nets and fishing tackle still tell unmistakable tales of the one trade in which every member of these communities is more or less engaged.

The winds blow strong, and the rain falls heavily. The frogs in the marshes behind the village fill the night air with the croakings of a thousand mouths, and the little bull-frogs sound their deep see-saw note during all the hours of darkness. The sun is often hidden by the heavy cloud-banks, and a subdued melancholy falls upon the moist and steaming land. The people, whom the monsoon has robbed of their occupation, lounge away the hours, building boats, and mending nets casually and without haste or concentrated effort. Four months must elapse before they can again put to sea, so there is no cause for hurry. They are frankly bored by the life they have to lead between fishing season and fishing season, but they are a healthy-minded and withal a law-abiding people, who do little evil even when their hands are idle.

Then the monsoon breaks, and they put out to sea once more, stretching to their paddles, and shouting in chorus as they dance across the waves to the fishing grounds. During this season numerous ugly and uncleanly steamboats tramp up the coast, calling at all the principal ports for the cargoes of dried fish that find a ready market in Singapore, and thus the fisher folk have no difficulty in disposing of their takes. Prices do not rank high, for a hundredweight of fish is sold on the East Coast for about six shillings and sixpence of our money, but the profits of a season are more than sufficient to keep a fisherman and his family in decency during the months of his inactivity. The shares which are apportioned to the working hands in each crew, and to the owners of the crafts and nets, are all determined by ancient custom. The unwritten law is clearly recognised and understood by all concerned, and thus the constant disputes which would otherwise inevitably arise are avoided. Custom—*Aädat*—is the fetish of the Malay. Before it even the *Hukum Sharä*, the Divine Law of the Prophet, is powerless, in spite of the professed Muhammadanism of the people. 'Let our children die rather than our customs,' says the vernacular proverb, and for once an old saw echoes the sentiment of a race.

The average monthly earnings of a fisherman is about sixteen shillings ($8), and though to our ideas this sounds but a poor return for all the toil and hardship he must endure, and the many risks and dangers which surround his avocation, to a simple people it is all-sufficient.

A fisherman can live in comfort on some three shillings a month, and wife and little ones can, therefore, be supported, and money saved against the close season, if a man be prudent. The owners of boats and nets receive far larger sums, but none the less they generally take an active part in the fishing operations. From one end of the coast to the other, the capitalist who owns many crafts, and lives upon the income derived from their hire, is almost unknown.

The fish crowd the shallow shoal waters, and move up and down the coast, during the whole of the open season, in great schools acres in extent. Occasionally their passage may be marked from afar by the flight of hungry sea-fowl hovering and flittering above them; the white plumage of the restless birds glints and flashes in the sunlight as they wheel and dip and plunge downwards, or soar upwards again with their prey. I have seen a school of fish beating the surface of the quiet sea into a thousand glistening splashes, as in vain they attempted to escape their restless pursuers, who, floating through the air above them, or plunging madly down, belaboured the water with their wings, and kept up a deafening chorus of gleeful screamings.

These seas carry almost everything that the salt ocean waters can produce. Just as the forests of the Peninsula teem with a life that is strangely prodigal in its profusion, and in the infinite variety of its forms, so do the waters of the China sea defy the naturalist to classify the myriad wonders of their denizens. The shores are strewn with shells of all shapes and sizes, which display every delicate shade of prismatic colour, every marvel of dainty tracery, every beauty of curve and spiral that the mind of man can conceive. The hard sand which the tide has left is pitted with tiny holes, the lairs of a million crabs and sea insects. The beaches are covered with a wondrous diversity of animal and vegetable growths thrown up and discarded by the tide. Seaweed of strange varieties, and of every fantastic shape and texture, the round balls of fibrous grass, like gigantic thistledowns, which scurry before the light breeze, as though endued with life, the white oval shells of the cuttle-fish, and the shapeless hideous masses of dead *medusæ*, all lie about in extricable confusion on the sandy shores of the East Coast.

In the sea itself all manner of fish are found; the great sharks, with their shapeless gashes of mouth set with the fine keen teeth; the sword-fishes with their barred weapons seven and eight feet long; the stinging ray, shaped like a child's kite, with its rasping hide and its two sharp bony prickers set on its long tail; the handsome *ténggiri*, marked like a mackerel, the first of which when taken are a royal perquisite on the Coast; the little smelts and red-fish; the thousand varieties that live among the sunken rocks, and are brought to the surface by lines six fathoms long; the cray-fish, prawns, and shrimps; and the myriad forms of semi-vegetable life that find a home in the tepid tropic sea, all these, and many more for which we have no name, live and die and prey upon each other along the eastern shores of the Peninsula.

Here may be seen the schools of porpoises—which the Malays name 'the racers'—plunging through the waves, or leaping over one another with that ease of motion, and that absence of all visible effort, which gives so faint an idea of the pace at which they travel. Yet when a ship is tearing through the waters at the rate of four hundred miles a day, the porpoises play backwards and forwards across the ploughing forefoot of the bow, and find no difficulty in holding their own. Here, too, is that monster fish which so nearly resembles the shark that the Malays call it by that name, with the added title of 'the fool.' It lies almost motionless about two fathoms below the surface, and when the fisher folk spy it, one of their number drops noiselessly over the side, and swims down to it. Before this is done it behoves a man to look carefully, and to assure himself that it is indeed the Fool, and not his brother of the cruel teeth who lies down below through the clear water. A mistake on this point means a sudden violent commotion on the surface, a glimpse of an agonised human face mutely imploring aid, the slow blending of certain scarlet patches of fluid with the surrounding water, and then a return to silence and peace, and the calm of an unruffled sea. But if it is indeed the Fool that floats so idly below them, the boatmen know that much meat will presently be theirs. The swimmer cautiously approaches the great lazy fish, which makes no effort to avoid him. Then the gently agitated fingers of a human hand are pressed against the monster's side just below the fins, and fish and man rise to the surface, the latter tickling gently, the former placid and delighted by the novel sensation. The swimmer then hitches one hand on to the boat in order to support himself, and continues the gentle motion of the fingers of his other hand, which still rests under the fin of his prey. The great fish seems too intoxicated with pleasure to move. It presses softly against the swimmer, and the men in the boat head slowly for the shore. When the shallow water is reached every weapon on board is plunged into the body of the Fool, and he is cut up at leisure.

Cray-fish also are caught by tickling all along the coast. The instrument used in this case is not the human hand, but a small rod, called a *jai*, to the end of which a rattan noose is fixed. The work is chiefly entrusted to little children, who paddle into the shallow water at points where the cray-fish are feeding, and gently tickle the itching prominent eyeballs of their victims. The irritation in these organs must be constant and excessive, for the cray-fish rub them gently against any object that presents itself, and when they feel the soothing friction of the rattan noose they lie motionless, paralysed with pleasure. The noose is gradually slipped over the protruding eyes, when it is drawn taut, and thus the great prawns are landed. Even when the strain has been taken too soon, and a cray-fish has escaped with one eyeball wrenched from its socket, it not uncommonly occurs that the intolerable irritation in its other eye drives it back once more to the rattan noose, there to have the itching allayed by the gentle friction.

Jelly-fish, too, abound on the East Coast. They come aboard in the nets, staring with black beady eyes from out the shapeless masses of their bodies, looking in the pale moonlight like the faces of lost souls, showing on the surface of the bottomless pit, casting despairing arms around their heads in impotent agony. The water which has sluiced over their slimy bodies is charged with irritating properties, such as drive a man to tear the very flesh from his bones in a fruitless attempt to allay the horrible itching. When the water dries, the irritation ceases, but at sea, and at night, when the dew falls like rain, and one is drenched to the skin by water from the nets, it is not easy for anything to become dry. Therefore one must suffer patiently till the boat puts back again at dawn.

These are some of the creatures which share with the Fisher Folk the seas of the East Coast, and hundreds of devices are used to capture them. Nets of all shapes and sizes, seine nets with their bobbing floats, bag nets of a hundred kinds, drop nets, and casting nets. Some are set all night, and are liberally sprinkled with bait. Some are worked round schools of fish by a single boat, which flies in its giant circle, propelled by a score of paddles dripping flame from the phosphorescence with which each drop of the Eastern sea is charged. Some are cautiously spread by the men in one boat, according to directions signalled to them by a second, from the side of which a diver hangs by one arm, listening intently to the motion of the fish, and judging with marvellous accuracy the direction which they are taking. Lines of all sorts, hooks of every imaginable shape, all the tricks and devices, which have been learned by hundreds of years of experience on the fishing grounds, are employed by the people of the East Coast to swell their daily and nightly takes of fish.

In the sheltered water of the Straits of Malacca, huge traps are constructed of stakes driven into the sea-bottom, and in these the vast majority of the fish are caught. But on the East Coast such a means of taking fish is forbidden by nature. A single day of monsoon wind would be sufficient to destroy and scatter far and wide the work of months, and so the Fisher Folk whose lot is cast by the waters of the China Sea, display more skill in their netting and lining than any other Peninsula Malays, for on these alone can they depend for the fish by which they live.

Their boats are of every size, but the shape is nearly the same in each case, from the tiny *kôlek* which can only hold three men, to the great *pûkat dâlam* or seine-boat, which requires more than a score of paddlers to work her. They are all made of *chêngal*, one of the hardest and toughest woods that is yielded by the jungles of the Peninsula. They all rise slightly at the stern and at the bows; they all are decked in with wide laths of bamboo; they all carry a mast which may be lowered or raised at will, and which seems to be altogether too tall and heavy for safety; they all fly under a vast spread of yellow palm-mat sail, the sight of which, as it fills above you, and you lie clutching the bulwark on the canting boat, while half the crew are hanging by ropes over the windward side, fairly takes your breath away; and all are so rigged that if taken aback the mast must part or the boat be inevitably capsized. But the Fisher Folk know the signs of the heavens as no others may know them, and when danger is apprehended the mast is lowered, the sail furled, and the boat headed for shore.

The real danger is when men are too eagerly engaged in fishing to note the signals which the skies are making to them. A party of Kĕlantan fisher folk nearly came by their death a year or two ago by reason of such carelessness. One of them is a friend of mine, and he told me the tale. Eight of them put to sea in a *jâlak* to troll for fish, and ran before a light breeze, with two score of lines trailing glistening spoon-baits in their wake. The fish were extraordinarily active, itself a pretty sure sign that a storm was not far off, but the men were too busy pulling in the lines, knocking the fish from the hooks with their wooden mallets, and trailing the lines astern again, to spare a glance at the sky or the horizon. Suddenly came the gust, striking, as do the squalls of the tropics, like the flat of a giant's hand. The mast was new and sound, the boat canted quickly, the water rose to the line of the bulwarks, paused, shivered, and then in a deluge plunged into the hold. A cry from the crew, a loud but futile shriek of directions from the owner, a splashing of released fish, a fighting flood of water, and the eight fishermen found themselves struggling in the arms of an angry sea.

The boat, keel uppermost, rocked uneasily on the waves, and the men, casting off their scant garments, made shift to swim to her, and climb up her slippery dipping side. The storm passed over them, a line of tropic rain, beating a lashing tattoo upon the white-tipped troubled waters; then a blinding downpour stinging on the bare brown backs of the shivering fishermen; and lastly a black shadow, lowering above a foam-flecked sea, driving quickly shorewards. Then came the sun, anxious to show its power after its temporary defeat. It beat pitilessly on the bare bodies of the men huddled together on the rocking keel of the boat. First it warmed them pleasantly, and then it scorched and flayed them, aided as it was by the fierce reflection thrown back from the salt waters. For a day and a night they suffered all the agonies of exposure in the tropics. Burning heat by day, chill airs at night, stiffening the uncovered limbs of the fishermen, who now half mad with hunger, thirst, and exhaustion, watched with a horrid fascination the great fins, which every now and then showed above the surface of the waters, and told them only too plainly that the sharks expected soon to get a meal very much to their liking.

On the second day Che' Leh, the owner of the boat, urged his fellows to attempt to right her by a plan which he explained to them, but at first the fear of the sharks held them motionless. At length hunger and thirst aiding Che' Leh's persuasions, they dropped off the boat, making a great splashing to scare the sharks, and after hours of cruel toil, for which their exhausted condition fitted them but ill, they succeeded in loosening the mast, and releasing the palm-leaf sail. Long pauses were necessary at frequent intervals, for the men were very weak. At last the sail floated upwards under the boat, and by a great effort the castaways succeeded in spreading it taut, so that the boat was half supported by it. Then, all pushing from one side, gaining such a foothold as the sail afforded them, they succeeded, after many straining efforts, in righting her. Slowly and painfully they baled her out, and then lay for many hours too inert to move.

Late on the third day they reached the shore, but they had been carried many miles down the coast to a part where they were unknown. The eight naked men presented themselves at a village and asked for food and shelter, but the people feared that they were fugitives from some *Râja's* wrath, and many hours elapsed before they received the aid of which they stood so sorely in need.

The beliefs and superstitions of the Fisher Folk would fill many volumes. They believe in all manner of devils and local sprites. They fear greatly the demons that preside over animals, and will not willingly mention the names of birds or beasts while at sea. Instead, they call them all *chêweh*—which, to them, signifies an animal, though to others it is meaningless, and is supposed not to be understanded of the beasts. To this word they tack on the sound which each beast makes in order to indicate what animal is referred to; thus the pig is the grunting *chêweh*, the buffalo the *chêwch* that says '*uak*,' and the snipe the *chêweh* that cries '*kek-kek*.' Each boat that puts to sea has been medicined with care, many incantations and other magic observances having been had recourse to, in obedience to the rules which the superstitious people have followed for ages. After each take the boat is 'swept' by the medicine man, with a tuft of leaves prepared with mystic ceremonies, which is carried at the bow for the purpose. The omens are watched with exact care, and if they be adverse no fishing boat puts to sea that day. Every act in their lives is regulated by some regard for the demons of the sea and air, and yet these folk are nominally Muhammadans, and, according to that faith, magic and sorcery, incantations to the spirits, and prayers to demons are all unclean things forbidden to the people. But the Fisher Folk, like other inhabitants of the Peninsula, are Malays first and Muhammadans afterwards. Their religious creed goes no more than skin deep, and affects but little the manner of their daily life.

All up and down the coast, from Sĕdĕli in Johor to the islands near Sĕnggôra, the Fisher Folk are found during the open season. Fleets of smacks leave the villages for the spots along the shore where fish are most plentiful, and for eight months in the year these men live and sleep in their boats. The town of Kuâla Trĕnggânu, however, is the headquarters of the fishing trade, as indeed it is of all the commercial enterprise on this side of the Peninsula. At the point where the

Trĕnggânu river falls into the sea, a sandy headland juts out, forming a little bay, to which three conical rocky hills make a background, relieving the general flatness of the coast. In this bay, and picturesquely grouped about the foot of these hills, the thatched houses of the capital, and the cool green fruit groves cluster closely. Innumerable fishing crafts lie at anchor, or are beached along the shore ; gaily-dressed natives pass hither and thither, engrossed in their work or play ; and the little brown bodies of the naked children fleck the yellow sands. Seen across the dancing waves, and with the appearance of motion which, in this steaming land, the heat-haze gives to even inanimate objects, this scene is indescribably pretty, shining and alive.

But at dawn the prospect is different. The background is the same, but the colour of the scene is less intense, though the dark waves have rosy lights in them reflected from the ruddy sky of the dawn. A slowly paling fire shines here and there upon the shore, and the cool land breeze blows seaward. Borne upon the wind come stealing out a hundred graceful, noiseless fishing smacks. The men aboard them are cold and sleepy. They sit huddled up in the stern, with their *sârongs* drawn high about their shoulders, under the shadow of the palm-leaf sail, which shows dark above them in the faint light of early morning. The only sound is the whisper of the wind in the rigging, and the song of the forefoot as it drives the water before it in little curving ripples. And so the fleet floats out and out, and presently is lost on the glowing eastern sky-line. At sundown the boats come racing back, heading for the sinking sun, borne on the evening wind, which sets steadily shorewards, and at about the same hour the great seine-boats, with their crews of labouring paddlers, beat out to sea.

So live they, so die they, year in and year out. Toiling and enduring, with no hope or wish for change of scene. Delighting in such simple pleasures as their poor homes afford; surrounded by beauties of nature, which they lack the soul to appreciate; and yet experiencing that keen enjoyment which is born of dancing waves, of pace, of action, and of danger, that thrilling throb of the red blood through the veins, which, when all is said and done, makes up more than half of the joy of living.

It was not always so with them, for within the memory of old men upon the Coast, the Fisher Folk were once pirates to a man. The last survivor of those who formed the old lawless bands was an intimate friend of mine own. When I last saw him, a day or two before his death in 1891, he begged that I would do him one final act of friendship by supplying him with a winding sheet, that he might go decently to his grave under the sods and the spear-grass, bearing thither a token of the love I bore him. It was a good shroud of fine white calico bought in the bazaar, and it cost more than a dollar. But I found it very willingly, for I remembered that I was aiding to remove from the face of the earth, and to lay in his quiet resting-place, the last Pirate on the East Coast.

THE STORY OF BÂYAN THE PAROQUET

> Said one among them, 'Surely not in vain
> My substance from the common Earth was ta'en
> And to this Figure moulded, to be broke,
> Or trampled back to shapeless Earth again.'
> *Omar Khayya'm.*

LIFE—meaning the life which animates the bodies of other people—is not priced high by the natives of the East Coast; but eight or nine years ago, it was held even more lightly than it is at present. Murder was frequently done for the most trivial causes, and a Malay often drew a knife, when an Englishman would have been content to drop a damn. Young Chiefs were wont to take a life or two from pure *gaieté de cœur*, merely to show that they were beginning to feel their feet, and were growing up brave and manly as befitted their descent. Such doings were not regarded altogether with disfavour by the boy's parents,—for, in a rude state of society, a Chief must be feared before he is loved, if his days are to be long in the land,—and some of the older men encouraged their sons to make a kill, much in the same spirit which animated parents in Europe half a century ago, when they put a finishing touch to the education of their children by sending them on the Grand Tour. Some fathers went even further than this, and Râja Haji Hamid once told me that he killed his first man when he was a child of eleven or twelve, his victim being a very thin, miserable-looking Chinaman, upon whom his father bade him try his 'prentice hand. The Chinaman had done no evil, but he was selected because he was feeble and decrepit, and would show no fight even if attacked by a small boy with a *kris*. Râja Haji told me that he botched the killing a good deal, but that he hacked the life out of the Chinaman at last, though the poor wretch, like Charles II., took an unconscionable time adying. Death to this Chinaman must have only been one degree less unpleasant than it was to the man who

> beyond the seas
> Was scraped to death with oyster shells
> Among the Carrabees.

The story of Bâyan the Paroquet, which I am about to tell, is another rather striking instance of the utter impunity with which the son of a Chief may take life, under the rule of a Native Prince in an Independent Malay State.

I first met Bâyan the Paroquet some six months before his death, when I was making my way across the Peninsula, *viâ* the Slim Mountains, in 1887. We were camped for the night at a spot in the jungle on the Pêrak side of the range, in a natural refuge, which has probably sheltered wayfarers in these forests ever since primitive man first set foot in the Peninsula. The place is called Bâtu Sâpor—the Stone Lean-to Hut —in the vernacular, and the name is a descriptive one. It is situated on the banks of the Brêseh, a little babbling stream which runs down to the Slim. The banks are high and shelving, but, on the top, they are flat, and it is here that the gigantic overhanging granite boulder stands, which gives the place its name. It is of enormous size, and is probably deeply embedded in the ground, for large trees have taken root and grow upon its upper surface. It projects some thirty feet over the flat bank, and then, shelving suddenly away to the ground, forms a stone roof, under which a score of men can camp with ease. The Pahang Prince, with whom I was travelling, unlike most of the men of that breed, was a very nervous person, and it was not without much persuasion that I had succeeded in inducing him to join me in my camp under the shadow of the great rock. He feared that it would topple over and crush us, nor was he completely reassured until Saiyid Jasin—the chief of his followers—a shrunken, wizened little man of many wiles, had propped the stone up with a slender sapling, over which he had duly recited certain magic incantations.

My attention was specially attracted to Bâyan the Paroquet, because he was the man who was told off to shampoo me after my march. He was a man of about forty years of age, thickset and large-limbed for a Malay, with a round bullet-shaped head, and a jolly smiling face.

Now, Bâyan the Paroquet was what is technically termed a *Pĕng-lipor Lâra*—or 'Soother of Cares,'— a class of men which is fast dying out in the Peninsula, as other mediæval landmarks become effaced. These people are simply the wandering bards and minstrels, who find their place in an Independent Malay State as naturally as did their prototypes in the countries of

Europe during the Middle Ages. They learn by rote some old-world tale, which has been transmitted by word of mouth through countless generations, and they wander from village to village, singing it for pay to the unlettered people, to whom these songs and stories represent the only literature which comes within their experience. Such minstrels are greatly loved by the villagers, who hold them in high honour, giving them hearty welcome, and the name by which they are known in the vernacular bears witness to the joy which they bring with them whithersoever they go. Bâyan's real name was Mat Sâman, but we always called him Bâyan—which means the Paroquet—because the tale which he sang told of the wonderful doings of a prince, who was transformed into a fabulous bird called the Bûrong Âgot, and whose attendants were the Paroquet and the Pied-robin (*Mûrai*). As he sat kneading me, as a baker kneads dough, he began to sing, and, that evening, and for many nights after, he sang his song to the *Râja* and myself, to the huge delight of our people.

There was also in camp at this time a boy named To' Mûda Long, who was the eldest son of one of the great up-country Chiefs. He was returning from Singapore with the *Râja*, to whom he had fled after some escapade of his had excited the paternal wrath. He was a nice-looking youngster, with a slight lisp, and a manner as soft as floss-silk, and he was always smartly dressed in pretty Malay garments. We travelled together for more than three months, and I got to know him pretty well, and took something of a liking to him. I knew, of course, that his manner to his own people was not always as gentle as that which he assumed when in the presence of the *Râja* or of myself, and during our progress through his father's district I heard many tales of his ill doings. To these, however, I attached but little importance, for Malays are very apt to malign a young Chief who, as they say, is born like a tiger cub, with teeth and claws, and may always be expected to do evil. Nevertheless, it would certainly never have occurred to me at that time that this mild-eyed, soft-spoken, silken-mannered, rather melancholy young man was capable of committing a peculiarly cruel, deliberate, and cold-blooded murder. Until one begins to understand them, one's Malay friends always seem to be breaking out in some new and unexpected place, to the intense mortification and surprise of people who attempt to judge Oriental character from a purely European standpoint.

The *Râja* and I journeyed through Pahang with great state and pageantry, our party increasing in bulk as we went along, after the manner of a snowball. The *Râja* and I were accommodated on a huge raft or floating house, and a perfect flotilla of boats accompanied us. At length, after many days spent in floating down the beautiful Pahang river, with the cool ripple of the water in our ears, and the ever-changing views to delight our eyes, we came in sight of Pĕkan, and, that night, we tied up about half a mile below the capital, at the landing-place which belonged to my travelling companion.

Thereafter followed negotiations, and interviews—made terrible by unearthly sweetmeats—much talk, and long waiting. Endless delays on the one side, stubborn patience that refused to be tired out on the other; and, as dawn was breaking on a certain Easter Sunday, I found myself, with a promise of a Treaty in my pocket, making my way out of the mouth of the river *en route* for Singapore. A fortnight later I was back at Pĕkan, to the no small disgust of my friend the Sultân and his people, but now I had quarters assigned to me in the royal village, and accordingly I saw but little of the *Râja* with whom I had formerly travelled, and the people who had accompanied him from the interior.

One day, about noon, I was aroused from sleep,— for, at Pĕkan, when first I lived there, all business was transacted at night, and no one of standing, who respected himself, thought of going to bed before eight o'clock in the morning, or of getting up till four in the afternoon. For Malays to wake one means that there is trouble, or that something untoward has occurred; for, in the Native States, slumber is respected,—as it ought to be, seeing how hard at times it is to come by,—and the European practice of being called in the morning, is a barbarous habit with which Malays have no sympathy. On this occasion there was a good reason for waking me, as news had just come in that To' Mûda Long had killed Bâyan the Paroquet, and as this had occurred in the compound of the *Râja*, with whom I had formerly travelled, and as he and the Sultân were on bad terms, there was room for fear that serious political complications would ensue. I, therefore, had occasion to inquire into the details of this murder, and this is what I learned.

To' Mûda Long, Bàyan the Paroquet, and the rest of the up-country natives, who had accompanied us down river to Pĕkan, remained in the *Râja's* enclosure to act as his body-guard and boat crew, and they had not been long at Pĕkan before the girls of the town began to send challenges to them, for Malay women dearly love a change, and these men were all strangers newly come among them. Nothing loth, the *Râja's* followers plunged hotly into the love intrigues which formed the principal interest in life to the people of Pĕkan, and the usual jealousies began to cause quarrels among them. Now, it chanced that To' Mûda Long and Bâyan both desired the same girl, and she, it would seem, preferred the Paroquet to the young Chieftain. Perhaps, his good voice, and the skill with which he sang the Song of the Bûrong Âgot, turned the balance in his favour, for Malay women love to be amused, and often favour those who are willing and able to amuse them. The girl was well born, and had many relatives, so To' Mûda Long could not make an open scandal by attempting to seize her by force, but his desire for her was hot in his breast, and he decided that Bâyan the Paroquet should die.

It only remained to seek a pretext for a quarrel, and this was easily found. In the afternoon the *Râja's* followers were accustomed to play *sêpak râga*, — a game which consists in kicking a round basket-work ball, made of rattan, from one to the other, without letting it fall to the ground. When it became dark, the players adjourned to the *Râja's bâlai* or hall, and some of them forgot to let down their trousers, which had been hitched up above their knees to leave their legs free while playing. Bâyan was one of the older men among the *Râja's* followers, and he, therefore, checked these youths; for, to enter a *Râja's bâlai* with bared knees is an act of rudeness. To' Mûda Long knew the custom, and, of course, his knees were covered, but when Bâyan spoke he leapt up and said:

'Arrogant one! Dost thou alone know the custom of kings? Thou art over clever at teaching men!'

And, drawing his *kris*, he made a murderous assault on Bâyan. The latter whipped his *kris* out, too, and it would have gone ill with To' Mûda Long, for Bâyan was a strong man and knew the use of his weapon, had not the older men, who were present, interfered to separate the combatants.

Next morning, Bâyan arose betimes, and, taking the long bamboos, in which water is stored and carried, he went down to the river to have his morning bath, and to fetch water for his house. He must have attached but little importance to the incident of the previous afternoon, for he went to the river unarmed, which was unusual in those days even for men who had no especial cause of quarrel. A Malay often judges the courage of his fellows by whether or no they are careful to be never separated from their weapons, and Europeans who, in humble imitation of Gordon, prefer to go about unarmed, make a great mistake, since a Malay is apt to interpret such action as being dictated by cowardice. Bâyan bathed in the river, filled his bamboos, and began to carry them to his house; but To' Mûda Long had been watching his opportunity, and he and two of his followers, all fully armed, had taken up a position in the middle of the path, by which Bâyan must pass back to his house.

'Thou wast over arrogant to me last night,' said To' Mûda Long as Bâyan approached, 'and now I will repay thee!'

'Have patience, To' Mûda, have patience,' said Bâyan. 'Thy servant did not speak to thee; it was the boys who were unmannerly, and thy servant, being an old man, did reprove them!'

'It is not for the like of thee to reprove men, and the said boys are my people, the sons of my loins. I will cover their shame!' said To' Mûda Long, for the wolf was determined to pick a quarrel with the lamb, bleat he never so wisely.

'Have patience, To' Mûda!' again cried poor Bâyan, but the words were hardly out of his mouth before To' Mûda Long struck at him with his spear, but missed him. Then, as Bâyan retreated step by step, defending himself with the clumsy bamboo from the deft spear thrusts, no more words passed between them.

At last the spear went home. '*Bâsah! Bâsah!* I have wetted thee!' cried To' Mûda Long, and he went in at his enemy, *kris* in hand, Bâyan beating him about the head with the now empty bamboo. When he got to close quarters, the deed was soon done, and the body of Bâyan the Paroquet, with seventeen rending wounds upon it, lay stark and hideously staring at the pure morning sky.

There was loud talk of blood-money, and equally

loud talk of reprisals, but nothing came of it; and though I often meet To' Mûda Long, who is as soft spoken and as gentle in his manners as ever, Bâyan's death was never revenged, and the fact that he ever lived and sang is now well-nigh forgotten, even by those who knew him, and loved to hear his tales.

A TALE OF A THEFT

.The voice of your complaining
  At the little ills you know,
The crumpled leaf that's paining,
  At the soil that's yours to sow,
At the exile from your caste-mates,
  At the toil, the sweat, the heat,
Bears down our cry against the Fates!
  We suff'rers round your feet!

To us the hardest lot you bear,
  Ere you pass Home again,
Were free and happy, bright and fair,
  If scaled against *our* pain.
We toil while others reap the fruit,
  We suffer nameless ills;
Our lives are withered to the root,
  By cruelty that kills.

Our very homes are not our own;
  Our children and our wives
Are riven from us, while we moan
  And labour out our lives.
They prison us in filthy sties
  Would shame your Christian Hell;
No ear there is to heed our cries,
  No tongue our pains to tell.
    The Very Bitter Cry of the Unprotected.

I HAVE said that the Malays, taken by and large, have no bowels. The story I am about to tell, illustrates this somewhat forcibly. The incident related happened on the East Coast, and I know it to be a fact. It is not a pleasant story, and any one who has a proud stomach, would do well not to read it, as it is calculated to make the gorge rise rebelliously.

In one of the States on the East Coast, there lived a *Râja*, who, though he was not the ruler of the country, was a man of standing, and was possessed of considerable power. This man owned much land, many cattle, several wives, and a number of slave-debtors, and his reputation for kindness and good-nature stood high among the people. It must be remembered, however, that the standard by which he was judged differs considerably from our own, otherwise, the things I am about to tell, would appear to accord but ill with the character he bore.

Upon a certain day a *kris* was stolen from him, and suspicion fastened upon one of his slave-debtors named Talib. The man was innocent of the theft, but his protestations were not believed, and he was forthwith consigned to the *Pĕn-jâra* or local gaol. The tedious formality of a trial was dispensed with, and nothing in the nature of the sifting of evidence was considered necessary. The stolen *kris* was the property of a Prince. That was enough; and Talib went to gaol forthwith, the Raja issuing an order—a sort of *lettre de cachet*—for his admittance. To European ears this does not sound very terrible. Miscarriages of justice, even in civilised lands, are not unknown, and in semi-barbarous countries they are, of course, all in the day's march. Unfortunately, however, an inspection of the gaols of Europe and of the Protected Native States, does not enable one to form a picture of the *Pĕn-jára* in Independent Malaya; and imprisonment in the former is not altogether the same thing as incarceration in the latter.

The gaol in which Talib was confined was situated in one of the most crowded portions of the native town. It consisted of two rows of cages, placed back to back, each one measuring some six feet in length, two feet in width, and five feet in height. These cages were formed of heavy slabs of wood, with intervals of some two inches in every eight, for the admission of light and air. The floors, which were also made of wooden bars, were raised about six inches from the ground; and the cages, which were twelve in number, were surrounded, at a distance of about two feet, by a solid wall, formed of slabs of wood joined closely one to another. Prisoners placed in these cells are never allowed to come out again, until the money payment has been made in satisfaction of the claim against them, or until kindly Death puts forth his hand to deliver them from worse pains than his.

Even this represents little to the European mind. Natives may perhaps live in a cage from necessity much as they often live in a boat from choice, and those who have never visited the prisoners in their captivity may think that no great suffering is inflicted upon them by such confinement. To fill in the picture one has to remember many things. No sanitary appliances of any kind are provided; no one ever cleans out the cages, or takes any steps to prevent the condition of the captives from being such as would disgrace that of a wild beast in a small travelling menagerie. The space between the floor and the ground, and the interval which separates the cells from the surrounding fence, is one seething, living mass of stinking putrefaction. Here in the tropics, under a brazen sun, all unclean things turn to putrid filthy life within the hour; and in a native gaol the atmosphere is heavy with the fumes and rottenness of the offal of years, and the reeking pungency of offal that is new. No ventilation can penetrate into the fetid airless cells, nor could the veriest hurricane purge the odours bred by such surroundings.

This then was the wretched life to which Talib was now condemned; nor did his agonies end here, for the gnawing pangs of hunger were added to his pains. He was handed over to the gentle care of the *Pĕr-tanda* or Executioner—an official who, in the Unprotected States, unites the kindly office of life-taker and torturer, with the hardly more humane post of gaoler. This man, like all his fellows, had been chosen for his physical strength, and his indifference to the sight of pain; and the calling, which he had pursued for years, had rendered the natural ferocity of his character abnormally brutal. He was, moreover, an Oriental official,—a class of worthies who require more supervision to restrain them from thieving, than do even the Chinese coolies in a gold mine, where the precious metal winks at one in the flickering candle-light. Needless to say, no attempt of any kind was made by the higher State officials to control the action of the *Pĕr-tanda*. During the months of the year in which the river was accessible to native crafts, he had the right to collect dues of rice and fish from all boats approaching the coast; but, during the close season of the north-east monsoon, no allowance of any kind was made to him for the board of the prisoners in his charge. Under these circumstances, perhaps, he was not greatly to blame if he perverted to his own use, and sold to all comers, the collections which he made during the open season, so that his household might not be without rice and raiment, during the dreary months when the hatches were down for the monsoon. Naturally, death, from slow and lingering starvation, was not an altogether uncommon incident in these dens of captivity, and one of Talib's first experiences was to witness the last agonies of a fellow prisoner in an adjoining cage. Talib himself was fed by a girl, who had been his sweetheart before his trouble fell upon him; and, though the pangs of hunger could not be completely allayed by the slender doles, which she daily saved from her own ration of rice and fish, he was not, for the time, exposed to actual danger of death from want.

The prisoner in the cage to his left was little more than a skeleton when Talib first entered the prison. He lay huddled up in a corner, with his hands pressed to his empty stomach and the sharp angles of his bones peeping through his bed-sores, motionless, miserable, but, let us hope, only half conscious of his misery. Talib saved a small portion of his own insufficient meal for this man, but the poor wretch was already too far gone for any such tardy aid to avail to save him. It was with difficulty that he could swallow the rice which Talib passed to him, in grudging handfuls, through the bars of his cell. When at last the food, by a superhuman effort, had been forced down his shrunken gullet, his enfeebled stomach refused to receive it, and violent spasms and vomiting followed, which seemed to rend his stricken frame, as a fierce wind rips through the palm-leaf sail of a native fishing-smack. In a day or two he became wildly delirious, and Talib then witnessed a terrible sight. A raving maniac in a well-ordered asylum, where padded walls and careful tendance do much to save the poor disordered soul from tearing its way through the frail casing of diseased flesh and bone, is a sight to shudder at, not to see! But in the vile cage in which this poor victim was confined, nothing prevented the maddened sufferer from doing himself any injury that it is possible for a demented wretch to do. With the strength of frenzy he dashed his head and body relentlessly against the unyielding bars of the cage. He fell back crushed and bleeding, foaming at the mouth with a bloody froth, and making inarticulate beast noises in his throat. Then, as the madness again took hold of him, shaking him as a terrier shakes a rat, he flung himself once more at the bars, and, after another fearful paroxysm, fell back inert upon the floor. For hours he lay exhausted, but wildly restless, too spent to struggle and too demented and tortured to be still. He moaned, he groaned, he cursed with horrid filthy words and phrases, bit as a dog bites in his madness, strove to gnaw the loathsome rags which had long ceased to cover his nakedness, and then again was still, save for the incessant rolling of his restless head, and the wilder motion of his eyes which glistened and flashed with fever. Just before dawn, when the chill air was making itself felt even in the fetid atmosphere of the place, his reason came back to him for a space, and he spoke to Talib in a thin, far-away voice, and with many gasps and sighs and pauses:

'Little Brother,' he said, 'Dost thou also watch? For not long now shall thy elder brother bear these pains. Hast thou any water? I thirst sore. No matter, it is the fate to which I was born. Brother, I stole five dollars from a Chief. I did it because my wife was very fair, and she abused me, saying that I gave her neither ornaments nor raiment. Brother, I was detected. I knew not then that it was my wife who gave the knowledge of my theft to the Chief,— he in whose household I was born and bred. He desired her, and she loved him, and now he has taken her to wife, I being as one already dead, and my wife being legally divorced from me. While she was yet bound to me, she sent to me food, by one of the Chief's slaves, and from him I learned the plot which had undone me. Brother, hast thou any water? I thirst sore, Little Brother. My mouth is hard and rough as the skin of the skate, and it is dry as the fish that has been smoked above the fire. Hast thou no water? Maimûnah! My wife! Water, I pray thee! Water! Water!—O mother! O mother! O mother of mine! Water, mother! Water! I die! I die! Mother! * * *'

His voice died away into inarticulate moaning, and, in an hour, he was dead.

Next morning his body was carried out for burial, and for a time his cage remained unoccupied.

In the cage on Talib's right, there was a man, so haggard, meagre, filthy, diseased, and brutal in his habits, that it was difficult to believe that he was altogether human. His hair fell in long, tangled, matted, vermin-infested shocks, almost to his waist. His eyes,—two burning pits of fierce fire,—were sunk deep into his yellow, parchment-coloured face. The cheek-bones were so prominent that they resembled the sharp edges of a *sĕládang's*[1] skull, and his temples stood out like the bosses on the forehead of a fighting ram. The dirt of ages clung in the thousand wrinkles and creases of his skin; and he hardly moved save to scratch himself fiercely, as a monkey tears at his flea-infested hide. A small ration of rice and fish was brought to him daily by an old and wrinkled hag,—his wife of other years,—who made a meagre living for him and for herself, by selling sweet-stuff from door to door. She came to him twice daily, and he tore ravenously at the food, eating it with horrible noises of animal satisfaction, while she cooed at him, through toothless gums, with many endearing terms, such as Malay women use to little children. Not even his misery and degradation had been able to kill her love, though its wretched object had long ceased to understand it, or to recognise her, save as the giver of the food he loved and longed for. He had been ten years in these cages, and had passed through the entire range of feeling, of which a captive in a Malay prison is capable. From acute misery to despair, from despair to stupid indifference, he had at length reached the stage which the Malays call *káleh*. It means insensibility, such as few can imagine or understand, and

---

[1] *Sĕládang* = wild buffalo of the Peninsula.

which is so bestial, that it reduces a feeling thinking human being to the level of an ape.

Talib himself had as yet reached only the first stage of his suffering, and the craving for one breath of fresh air grew and grew and gathered strength, until it became an overmastering longing that day and night cried out to be satisfied. At last he could restrain the desire no longer, and, reckless of the consequences, he told the *Pĕr-tanda* that, if he could be taken to a place a day's journey up the river, he could set his hand upon the missing *kris* which he had hidden there. He was perfectly aware that the *kris* was not, and never had been, buried in that place, for he knew as little of it as the *Pĕr-tanda* himself. He could forsee that his failure to find it would be followed by worse tortures, but he heeded not. He would breathe the free fresh air once more, would look again up on the clear blue vault of heaven overhead, would hear the murmur of running water, the sighing of the wind through the fruit trees, and would see, smell, hear, and feel, all the sights, the scents, the sounds, and the surroundings that he loved and longed for so keenly.

On a certain day he was taken up river, to the place he had named, but the stinking reek of the cell seemed to cling about him, and the fresh air was to him made foul by it. The search was fruitless of course, he was beaten by the boatmen, who had had their toil for nothing, and sore and bleeding he was placed once more in his hated cage, with the added pain of heavy irons to complete his sufferings. An iron collar was riveted about his neck, and attached by heavy links to chains passed about his waist, and to rings around his ankles. The fetters galled him, prevented him from lying at ease in any attitude, and doubled the number of his bed-sores. The filthy bloated flies buzzed around him now in larger numbers, feasting horribly on his rottenness, and he himself was sunk in stupid, wide-eyed despair.

A Chinese lunatic had been placed in the vacant cage on his left, a poor mindless wretch, who cried out to all who visited the prison, that he had become a Muhammadan, vainly hoping thereby to meet with some small pity from the worshippers of Allah, the Merciful, the Compassionate. The bestial habits of this wretched creature, whose madness was intensified by his misery, and by his surroundings, made Talib's life more keenly horrible than ever; but he himself was now fast sinking into the stolid, animal indifference of his right-hand neighbour. I saw him, exactly as I have described him, some two years ago, and, unless kindly death has set him free, he has now, I do not doubt, reached the happy condition of *kâleh*.

If the men suffer thus, what are the pains endured by tender women and by little children? It makes one sick to think of it! And yet, all these things happened and are happening to-day, within shouting distance of Singapore, with its churches, and its ballrooms, its societies for the prevention of cruelty, its missionaries, its discontented exiled Europeans, its high standards, its poor practice, its loud talk, and its boasted civilisation.

IN A CAMP OF THE SĚMANGS

> The paths are rough, the trails are blind
>   The Jungle People tread;
> The yams are scarce and hard to find
>   With which our folk are fed.
> We suffer yet a little space
>   Until we pass away,
> The relics of an ancient race
>   That ne'er has had its day.
>
> *The Song of the Last Sěmangs.*

THE night was closing in apace as I and my three Malay companions pushed our way through the underwood which overgrew the narrow wood path. We were marching through the wide jungles of the Upper Pêrak valley, which are nearer to the centre of the Malay Peninsula than any point to which most men are likely to penetrate. Already the noisy crickets and tree beetles were humming in the boughs above our heads, and the voices of the bird folk had died down one by one until now the monotonous note of the night-jar alone smote upon our ears. The colour was dying out of the leaves and grasses of the jungle, and all things were assuming a single sombre shade of black, the trees and underwood becoming merged into one monstrous shapeless mass, bulking big in the gathering darkness.

We had been delayed all day, by constantly going astray on the innumerable faint tracks, which, in this part of the country, begin nowhere in particular, and end nowhere at all. The jungle-dwelling tribes of Sĕmang, who alone inhabit these woods, guard their camps jealously, for, until lately, they were often raided by slave-hunting bands of Malays and Sâkai. To this end they do all that woodcraft can suggest to confuse the trails which lead to their camps, making a very maze of footpaths, which serve but as a faint guide to strangers in these forests.

The Sĕmang are the survivors of a very ancient race of negrits, remnants of which are still to be found scattered over Eastern Asia, and may be supposed to be the first family of our human stock that ever possessed these glorious lands. In appearance they are like African negroes seen through the reverse end of a field-glass. They are sooty black in colour; their hair is short and woolly, clinging to the scalp in little crisp curls; their noses are flat, their lips protrude, and their features are those of the pure negroid type. They are sturdily built, and well set upon their legs, but they are in stature little better than dwarfs. They live by hunting, and have no permanent dwellings, camping in little family groups, wherever, for the moment, game is most plentiful, or least difficult to come by.

It was a fire from the camp of a band of these little people, which presently showed red in the darkness a few yards away from us, just when we were despairing of finding either a shelter for the night or a meal with which to satisfy the pangs of hunger, that a twelve hours' march had caused to assail us. We pushed on more rapidly when the gleam of welcome light showed us that men were at hand, and presently we emerged upon a tiny opening in the forest, in the centre of which the Sĕmang camp was pitched. The shelters of these people were rough enough to deserve no better name. They consisted of three or four lean-to huts, formed of plaited palm leaves, propped crazily on rudely trimmed uprights, and round the fire, in the centre of the camp, a dozen squalid aborigines were huddled together. We approached very cautiously, and when I had been seen and recognised, for I was well known in these parts, the sudden panic, which our presence had occasioned, subsided quickly, and we were made free of the encampment and all that it contained.

Hunger is a good sauce, and I ate with a satisfaction which has often been lacking at a dinner table at home, of the rude meal set before me. A cool green leaf of the wild banana was spread for me, and on it were laid smoking yams and other mealy jungle roots, which fill one, as young turkeys are filled during their rearing; a few fish, fresh caught in the stream and cooked over the fire in the cleft of a split stick, and the meat of some nameless animal—monkey I feared—which had been dried in the sun until it was as hard as a board, eked out the curious meal. I did full justice to the roots and fish, but prudently left the doubtful meat alone, and when the cravings of my hunger were appeased, I began to make advances to my hosts.

First I produced a palm-leaf bag holding about four pounds of coarse Chinese rock salt, and bade the Sĕmang gather round and partake. The whole contents of the bag were emptied out on to a leaf with minute care lest one precious grain should be lost, and then the naked aborigines gathered round and feasted. These jungle dwellers lack salt in their daily food, and look upon it as a luxury, much as a child regards the contents of a *bon-bon* box. With eager fingers they clutched the salt, and conveyed it to their mouths in handfuls. This coarse stuff would take the skin off the tongues of most human beings who attempted to eat it in this way, but I suppose that nature gives the Sĕmang the power to take in abnormally large quantities of salt at one time, because his opportunities of eating it in small daily instalments are few and far between. In an incredibly short time the four pounds of salt had disappeared, and when the leaf had been divided up, and licked in solemn silence, the Chief of the family, an aged, scarred, and deeply wrinkled negrit, turned to me with a sigh and said—

'It is very sweet, this salt that thou hast given us. Hast thou tobacco also, that we may smoke and rest?'

I produced some coarse Japanese tobacco which I had brought with me for the purpose, and when cigarettes had been rolled, with green leaves for wrappers, we all squatted around the fire, for the night was chilly up here in the foothills, and the silence of sated appetite and rested limbs fell gently upon us.

The eyes of one who dwells in the untrodden

places of the earth are apt to grow careless of the picturesque aspect of his surroundings. He is often too busy following the track beneath his feet, or observing some other such thing, which is important for his immediate well-being, to more than glance at the beauties which surround him. Often, too, his heart is so sick for a sight of the murky fogs, and drizzle-damped pavements of London, or for the ordered green fields and hedgerows of the pleasant English country, that he does not readily spare more than a grudging tribute of admiration to the scenes which surround him in his exile. To-night, however, as I sat and lay by the crackling logs, I longed, as I had often done before, to possess that power which transfers the sights we see to paper or to canvas. Around us the forest rose black and impenetrable, the shadows deepened by the firelight of the camp. In the clear sky overhead the glorious Eastern stars were shining steadfastly, and at our feet a tiny stream pattered busily on the pebbles of its bed. Around the fire, and reddened by its light, sat or lay my three Malays, bare to the waist, but clothed in their bright *sârongs* and loose short trousers. The Sĕmang, of both sexes and all ages, coal black, save where the gleams of the fire painted them a dull red, and nude, save for a narrow strip of coarse bark cloth twisted round their loins, lay on their stomachs with their chins propped upon their elbows, or squatted on their hams, smoking placidly. A curious group to look upon we must have been could any one have seen us: I, the European, the white man, belonging to one of the most civilised races in the Old World; the Malays, civilised too, but after the fashion of unchanging Asia, which differs so widely from the restless progressive civilisation of the West; and, lastly, the Sĕmangs, squalid savages, nursing no ambitions save those prompted by their empty stomachs, with no hope of change or improvement in their lot, and yet representing one of the oldest races in the world—a race which, though it first possessed the East, with all its possibilities and riches, could utilise none of them, and whose members carry in their eyes the melancholy look of dumb animals, which, when seen on the human countenance, denotes a people who are doomed to speedy extinction, and who, never since time began, have had their day or have played a part in human history.

Tobacco upon the mind of man has much the same effect as that which hot water has upon tea-leaves, or, indeed, as that which that beverage itself has on the majority of women. It calls out much that, without its aid, would remain latent and undeveloped. For human beings this means words, and, while we dignify our own speech over our tobacco by the name of conversation, we are apt to dispose of that of the ladies round a tea-table by labelling it gossip. Among a primitive people conversation means either broken remarks about the material things of life—the food which is sorely needed and is hard to come by, the boat which is to be built, or the weapon which is to be fashioned—or else it takes the form of a monologue, in which the speaker tells some tale of his own or another's experiences to those who sit and listen. Thus it was that upon this evening, as we clustered round the fire in this camp of the Sĕmangs, the aged patriarch, who had praised the 'sweetness' of my salt, lifted up his voice and spoke in this wise.

'The jungles are growing empty now, *Tûan*, and many things are changed since the days when I was a boy roaming through the woods of the Plus valley with my father and my two brothers. Now we live in these poor jungles of the Upper Pêrak valley, where the yams and roots are less sweet and less plentiful than in our former home, and where the fish-traps are often empty, and the game wild and scarce. Does the *Tûan* ask why then we quitted the valley of the Plus, and the hills of Lĕgap, where once our camps were pitched? The *Tûan* knows many things, and he has visited the forests of which I speak, why then does he ask our reason? It was not for love of these poor hunting grounds that we quitted the Plus valley, but because we loved our women-folk and our little ones. The *Tûan* knows the tribe of Sâkai who have their homes in the Plus, but does he not know also that they entered into a compact with the Malays of Lâsak to aid in hunting us through the woods and selling all of our people whom they could catch into slavery? We of the forests had little fear of the Malays, for we could make blind trails that they could never follow, and could hide our camps in the shady places, where they could never find them. The Malays were wont, when they could trace us, to surround our camps at nightfall, and attack when the dawn was about to break, but many and many a time, when we were so surrounded, we made shift by night to escape from the circle which hemmed us in. How did we win out? What then are the trees made for? Has the *Tûan* never heard of the bridges of the forest people that the Malays call *tâli těnau?* When darkness was over the forest, the young men would ascend the trees, and stretch lines of rattan from bough to bough, over the places where the trees were too far apart for a woman to leap, and when all was ready, we would climb into the branches, carrying our cooking-pots and all that we possessed, the women bearing their babies at their breasts, and the little children following at their mothers' heels. Thus, treading shrewdly on the lines of rattan, we would pass from tree to tree, and so escape from our enemies. What does the *Tûan* say? That it is difficult and hazardous to walk by night on slender lines stretched among the tree-tops? No, the matter was easy. Where there is room to set a foot, why need a man fear to fall? And thus we baffled the Malays, and won our freedom. But when the Sâkai dogs aided the Malays, matters were changed indeed. They would sit in the tree-tops, the whole night through, calling one to another when we tried to break away; and, by day, they would track our foot-prints through places where no Malay might follow; and no trail was so blind but that the Sâkai could see the way it tended. Men said that they served the Malays in this manner that thereby they might preserve their own women-folk from captivity. But I know not. The Sâkai live in houses, and plant growing things—like the Malays. They know much of the lore of the forest, but many secrets of the jungle which are well known to us are hidden from their eyes. Yea, even though the fair valley of the Plus is now possessed by them, and the mountain of Korbu is now *their* home as it was once our own, the spirits of the hills and streams are still our friends, and they teach not their secrets to the strangers. How should it not be so? Our tribe springs from the mountain of Korbu, and the hills of Lĕgap; theirs from the broad forests towards the rising sun, beyond the Kinta valley. No tribe but ours knows of the forests at the back of Gûnong Korbu, nor of the doom, which, in the fulness of time, will fall upon the Sâkai. Beyond that great peak, in the depths of the silent forest places, there lives a tribe of women, fair of face and form, taller than men, paler in colour, stronger, bolder. This is the tribe that is to avenge us upon those who have won our hunting grounds. These women know not men; but when the moon is at the full they dance naked, in the grassy places near the salt-licks, where the passing to-and-fro of much game has thinned the forest. The Evening Wind is their only spouse, and through Him they conceive and bear children. Yearly are born to them offspring, mostly women-folk whom they cherish even as we do our young; but if, perchance, they bear a manchild, the mother slays it ere it is well-nigh born. Thus live they, and thrive they, ever increasing and multiplying, and their bows and blow-pipes are sometimes found by us in the deep hollows of the woods. Larger are they than those we use, more beautifully carved, and, moreover, they are of a truer aim. But woe to the man who meets these women, or who dares to penetrate into the woods in which they dwell, for he will surely die unless the ghosts give speed to his flight. Of all this tribe, I alone have seen these women, and that when I was a young hunter, many

many moons agone. I and two others, my brothers, when hunting through the forest, passed beyond the limits of our own woods, following the halting tracks of a wounded stag. After much walking, and eager following of the trail, for the camp was hungry lacking meat, we found the stag lying near a brook, killed by a larger arrow than the bow we carry throws, and, at the same moment, we heard a loud, threatening cry in a strange tongue. Then I, looking up, beheld a gigantic form, as of a pale-skinned woman, breaking through the jungle, some two hundred elbow-lengths away, and, at the same moment, my elder brother fell pierced by an arrow. I stayed to see no more, but ran, with all my young blood tingling with fear, leaving my brothers and the slaughtered stag, tearing through the thickets of thorn, but never feeling them rend my skin, nor ever stopped to catch my breath or drink, until, all wounded and breathless, covered with blood and sweat-like foam, I half fell, half staggered to the camp of mine own people. Thereafter, for long days, I lay 'twixt life and death, screaming in fear of the dreadful form I ever fancied was pursuing me. My brothers never again returned to camp, and I alone am left to tell the tale.'

The old man ceased his weird story, the fear of what he thought he had seen still apparently strong upon him. He certainly believed what he said, as also did every person present, with the exception of my own sceptical self, and I have often tried to find some reasonable explanation for the story. I have not succeeded, for, even in the wildest parts of the Peninsula, the aborigines do not shoot one another on sight, whatever they may do to bands of marauding Malays, nor do serious

CAMP OF THE SĕMANGS

quarrels ever arise between them over the division of a little fresh meat. Judging by the scared look in his eyes, as he told the story, the old Sĕmang had felt the fear of imminent death very close at hand that day long ago in the quiet forests at the back of Gûnong Korbu. His brethren, too, must undoubtedly have been killed by some one or something, and perhaps the old-world tradition of the Amazons, furnished to the mind of the survivor the most natural explanation of the catastrophe.

A dozen years and more have slipped away since I heard this tale, told in the fire-light of the Sĕmang camp, in the Upper Pêrak valley, and now there is a trigonometrical survey station on the summit of Korbu. It is true that the surveyors employed there have made no mention in their reports of the Amazons of the neighbourhood, and the Sâkai are still living in prosperity, in spite of the impending doom, which the old Sĕmang foretold for them. None the less, however, I hold to the belief that my informant actually did see something weird and uncanny at the back of Gûnong Korbu; and that the keen eyes of a jungle-dwelling Sĕmang should not be able to clearly recognise anything their owner could encounter in the forests of the Peninsula, is, in itself, a miracle.

'HIS HEART'S DESIRE'

> They wrench my back on a red-hot rack,
>   They comb my nerves with wire,
> They poison with pain the blood of my brain
>   Till the Devils of Devilry tire;
> They spit from Above on the name of my Love,
>   They call my Love a liar;
> But they can't undo the joy I knew
>   When I knew my Heart's Desire.
>   *The Song of the Lost Soul.*—ANON.

WHERE and when these things happened does not signify at all. The East Coast is a long one, and the manners of the Malay *Râjas* who dwell thereon have suffered but little change for centuries. Thus, both in the matter of time and of space, there is a wide choice, and plenty of exercise may be given to the imagination. The facts anyway are true, and they were related, in the watches of the night, to a White Man—whose name does not matter—by two people, with whose identity you also have no concern. One of the latter was a man whom I will call Âwang Îtam, and the other was a woman whose name was Bêdah, or something like it. The place in which the tale was told was an empty sailing boat which lay beached upon a sandbank in the centre of a Malay river, and, as soon as the White Man had scrambled up the side, the dug-out, which had brought him, sheered off and left him.

He had come to this place by appointment, but he did not know precisely whom he was to meet, as the assignation had been made in the secret native fashion, which is as different from the invitation card of Europe as most things in the East are different from white men's gear. Twice that day his attention had been very pointedly called to this deserted sailing boat; once by an old crone who was selling sweetstuff from door to door, and once by a young chief who had stopped to speak to him, while passing up the street of the native town. By both of these some reference had been made to the moon-rise and to 'a precious thing'; and this was enough to show the White Man that something was to be learned, seen, or experienced by going to the deserted sailing boat at the rising of the moon.

The Malays who were with him feared a trap, and implored him not to go alone; but the White Man did not fancy that treachery was likely just then, and, in any case, he was anxious for the adventure, and could not afford to let his people think that he was afraid. The man who, dwelling alone among Malays in an unsettled country, shows the slightest trace of fear, signs his own death-warrant. No people are more susceptible to 'bluff,' and, given a truculent bearing, and a sufficiency of bravado, a coward may pass for a brave man in many a Malay State.

The decks of the boat were wet with dew and drizzle, and she smelt abominably of ancient fish cargoes which she had carried before she was beached.

A light rain was falling, and the White Man crept along the side until he reached the stern, which was covered with a roofing of rotten palm-leaf mats. Through the rents at the stern he could see the moon rising like a great red ball, throwing a broad wave of dancing light along the reaches of the river. Then he squatted down, rolled a cigarette, and awaited developments.

Presently the soft *splish, whisp! splash, whisp!* of a single paddle came to his listening ear; and, a moment later, a girl's form, standing erect on the vessel's side, showed distinctly in the growing moonlight. She called softly to know if anybody was aboard, and the White Man answered equally cautiously. She then turned and whispered to some unseen person in a boat moored alongside, and, after some seconds, she came towards the White Man and said:

'There is one who would speak with thee, *Tûan*, but he cannot climb up the ship's side. He is like a dead man—unless one lifts him, how can he move? Will the *Tûan*, therefore, aid him to ascend into the ship?'

The White Man loosened his pistol in its holster, covertly, that she might not see, and stepped cautiously to the place where the boat appeared to be moored, for he, too, began to fear a trap. What he saw over the side reassured him. The dug-out was of the smallest, and it had only one occupant. He was a man who, even in the dim moonlight, showed the sharp angles of his bones. He had a peculiarly drawn and shrunken look, and the skin was stretched across his hollow cheeks like the goat-hide on a drum-face.

The White Man leaped down into the boat, and, aided by the girl, he lifted the man on board. Then, painfully and very slowly, the latter crept aft, going on all fours like some unclean animal, until he had reached the shelter in the stern. The girl and the White Man followed, and they all three squatted down on the creaking bamboo decking. The man sat, all of a heap, moaning at short intervals, as Malays moan when the fever holds them. The girl sat unconcernedly preparing a quid of betel-nut from its four ingredients, and the White Man inhaled his cigarette and waited for them to speak. He was trying to get the hang of the business, and to guess what had caused two people, whom he did not know, to seek an interview with him in this weird place, at such an untimely hour.

The girl, the moonlight told him, was pretty. She had a small, perfectly shaped head, a wide smooth forehead, neat, glossy hair, bright, laughing eyes, with eyebrows arched and well-defined, 'like the artificial spur of a fighting cock,' and the pretty little hands and feet which are so common among all well-born Malay women. The man was hideous. His shrunken and twitching face with its taut skin, and his utterly broken, degraded, and decrepit appearance were indescribably horrible, and the flickering of the moonlight, through the torn mat overhead, only added to the grotesqueness of his figure.

At length the girl looked up at the White Man, and spoke:

'The *Tūan* knows Âwang Îtam?' she asked. Yes, the White Man knew him well, but had not seen him for some months.

'This is he,' she said, pointing to the abject figure by her side, and her listener felt as though she had struck him across the face. When last he had seen Âwang Îtam, he was one of the best favoured of the King's Youths, a fine, upstanding youngster, dressed in many-coloured silks, and with an amount of side and swagger about him, which would have amply sufficed for a regiment of Her Majesty's Guards. Now he half lay, half sat, on the damp decking, the most pitiful wreck of humanity that the White Man had ever seen. What had befallen him to cause so fearful a change? I will tell you the tale, in my own words, as the White Man learned it from him and Bêdah, as they sat talking during the watches of that long night.

In every Independent Malay State, there is a gang of fighting men, which watches over the person of the King and acts as his bodyguard. It is recruited from the sons of the chiefs, nobles, and men of the well-bred classes; and its members follow at the heels of the King whenever he goes abroad, paddle his boat, join with him in the chase, gamble unceasingly, do much evil in the King's name, slay all who chance to offend him, and flirt lasciviously with the girls within the palace. They are always ready for anything from 'pitch-and-toss to manslaughter,' and no Malay king has to ask twice in their hearing 'Will nobody rid me of this turbulent priest?' Their one aim in life is to gain the favour of their master, and, having won it, to freely abuse their position. As the Malay proverb has it, they carry their master's work upon their heads, and their own under their arms, and woe betide those who are not themselves under the immediate protection of the King, that chance throws in their way. Sometimes they act as a kind of irregular police force, levying *chantage* from those whom they detect in the commission of an offence; and, when crime is scarce, they often exact blackmail from wholly innocent people by threatening to accuse them of some ill-deed, unless their goodwill is purchased at their own price. They are known as the *Bûdak Râja* —or King's Youths—and are greatly feared by the people, for they are as reckless, as unscrupulous, as truculent, and withal as gaily dressed and well born a gang of young ruffians, as one would be like to meet in a long summer's cruise.

Âwang Îtam had served the King for several years as one of the *Bûdak Râja*, but his immediate chief was Saiyid Ûsmân, a youngster who was also one of the King's Youths, and was usually spoken of as Tûan Bàngau. Âwang had been born and bred in the house of which Tûan Bàngau's father was the head, and, though in accordance with the immutable Malay custom, Âwang always spoke of himself as 'thy servant' when he addressed Tûan Bàngau, the relations which subsisted between them more nearly resembled those of brothers, than those which we recognise as being proper to master and servant. They had crawled about the floor of the women's apartments in company, until they were old enough to play in the open air; they had played *pôrok* and *tûju lûbang*, and all the games known to Malay children, still in company; they had splashed about in the river together, cooling their little brown bodies in the running water; they had often eaten from the same plate, and had slept side by side on the same mat spread in the verandah. Later, they had been circumcised on the same day, and, having thus entered upon man's estate, they had together begun to participate in the life of dissipation which every court-bred Malay boy regards as his birthright. Thus they had gone astraying after strange women, gambling and quarelling with the other youths, but still in company, and with their old love for one another unaltered. They had been duly entered as members of the King's Youths, and had proved themselves not to be the least reckless and truculent of those who form that ruffianly gang, but they had chiefly used their position to carry on their love intrigues with greater freedom and daring. Both were handsome, dashing, fearless, swaggering, gaily-dressed boys, and many were the girls within the palace, and the town which lay around it, who cast loving eyes upon them. Âwang, however, cared little for this, for, by the irony of that Fate which always directs that men should fall in love with the wrong women, and *vice versâ*, his heart was eaten up with a fiery desire for a girl who was a *jâmah-jâmah-an*, or casual concubine of the King, and who resolutely declined to have ought to do with him. Nevertheless, the moth still fluttered around the candle, and Âwang never missed an opportunity of catching a passing glimpse of the object of his longing. It was an evil day for both Âwang Îtam and Tûan Bângau, however, when, as they swaggered past the palace-fence, seeking to peep at this girl, they were seen by the King's daughter, Tŭngku Ûteh, and a desire was straightway born in her breast for the young and handsome Saiyid.

In the East, love affairs develop quickly; and that very day Âwang Îtam again saw Iang Mûnah, the girl whom he had loved so long and so hopelessly, and by a flash of an eye-lid was informed that she had that to tell him which it concerned him to know. When both parties desire a secret interview many difficulties may be overcome, and that evening Âwang whispered into the ear of Tûan Bângau that 'the moon was about to fall into his lap.'

'I dreamed not long since,' said Tûan Bângau, 'that I was bitten by a very venomous snake!' And then Âwang knew that his friend was ready for any adventure.

To dream of a snake bite, among any of the people of the Far East, means that ere long the dreamer will receive generous favours from some lady who is either of exalted rank, or of most surpassing beauty. The greater the venom of the snake, the brighter, it is believed, are the qualities with which the dreamer's future mistress is endowed. It is not only in Europe, that venom enters into the soul of a man by reason of a woman, and this is, perhaps, the explanation of how this dream comes to bear this peculiar interpretation.

Tûan Bângau's position was a curious one. He did not desire Tŭngku Ûteh for herself; she was his King's daughter, and the wife of a royal husband; and his duty and his interest alike forbade him to accept her advances. If his intrigue with her was discovered, he was a ruined, if not a dead man, and, moreover, he was at this time devoted to another girl, whom he had recently married. The challenge which had been conveyed to him, however, was one which, in spite of all these things, his code of honour made it impossible for him to refuse. The extreme danger, which lay in such an intrigue, gave him no choice but to accept it. That was his point of view, 'His honour rooted in dishonour stood,' and no self-respecting Malay, brought up in the poisonous atmosphere of an Independent Malay State, could admit of any other opinion.

With Âwang Îtam things were different. I have already said that he was passionately in love with Iang Mûnah, and he knew that he would at length win his Heart's Desire. He would accompany his chief on his nocturnal visits to the palace, and, while Tûan Bângau wooed the Princess, the handmaiden would give herself to him. He felt the 'blood run redder in every vein' at the bare thought, and he was the eager and impatient lover when the twain crept into the palace in the noon of the night.

They effected their entrance by a way known only to themselves, and left by the same means before the breaking of the dawn, passing to their quarters in the guard-house, through the slumbering town, and lay sleeping far into the day. For more than a month they paid their secret visits unobserved by any save those whom they sought, and by the old crone who unbarred the door for them to enter; but, upon a certain night, they narrowly escaped detection. The King, like many Malay *Râjas*, kept curious hours. Sometimes, he slept all day, sometimes he slept all night; some days he went to rest at noon, to awake at midnight; and, on such occasions, he often wandered about the palace alone, pouncing upon ill-doers, like the lion which seeketh whom it may devour. In this way he chanced upon Tûan Bàngau and Âwang Îtam, but they had fled from the palace before he had learned who they were, and who were the girls whom they had come to seek.

After this the meetings ceased for a space, but Tŭngku Ûteh was not to be so easily baulked, and a taunting message soon brought Tûan Bàngau once more to her feet. The meetings, however, no longer took place within the palace itself, the lovers meeting and passing the night in a wood-shed within the fence of the royal enclosure.

Things had gone on in this way for some time when Tŭngku Ûteh began to weary of the lack of excitement attending the intrigue. Like many Malay women she regarded it as a reproach to a girl if no man desired her, and the longing became greater and greater to show her partner and her immediate *entourage* that she also was wooed and loved. She had an affection for Tûan Bàngau, and admired him as a lover and a man, but even this could not restrain the growing longing for notoriety. Perhaps she hardly realised how grave would be the consequences; perhaps she struggled against the impulse; who can say? The fact remains that her lover was sacrificed, as many a man has been before and since, upon the altar of a woman's ungovernable vanity.

One night, when the yellow dawn was splashing the gray in the East, and the thin smoke-like clouds were hurrying across the sky, like great night fowls winging their homeward way, Tûan Bàngau awoke and found Ûteh sitting beside him with his *kris* and girdle in her hands. She had taken them from his pillow as he slept, and no persuasions on his part could induce her to return them. While he yet sought to coax her into foregoing her resolve, she leaped to her feet, and, with a sweet little laugh, disappeared in the palace, and Tûan Bângau returned homeward with Âwang Îtam, each knowing that now indeed their hour was come.

Once inside her own apartments, Tŭngku Ûtch placed the *kris* ostentatiously at the head of her sleeping mat, and then composed herself calmly to enjoy the tranquil slumber, which in the West is erroneously supposed to be the peculiar privilege of the just. Next day, the *kris* had been seen and recognised, but her father and mother received nothing but taunts from Ûteh in reply to their inquiries. What her object was is difficult for the European mind to appreciate, for it must be distinctly remembered that she had no quarrel with Tûan Bângau. A Malay woman, however, is very far from regarding the possession of a lover as a disgrace: in this case, Ûteh's vanity was gratified by the intrigue becoming known. To obtain this even the sacrifice of her lover did not seem too heavy a price to pay.

The King's anger knew no bounds when he heard of what had occurred, and physical punishment was, of course, the only means of covering his shame, which occurred to his primitive and unoriginal imagination. His position, however, was a difficult one. Tûan Bângau was a member of a very powerful clan; he was also a Saiyid, and the King feared that the fanaticism of his people would be aroused if he openly slew a descendant of the Prophet Muhammad. Âwang Îtam, whose intrigue had also become known, was arrested, carried into the palace, and all trace was lost of him for months. Iang Mûnah also disappeared from among the women; but to Tûan Bângau not a word was said, and never by sign or gesture was he allowed to guess that his crime was known to the King.

One day the King went a hunting, and took his way up a small stream which was totally uninhabited. Tûan Bângau was of the party, and those who went with them were all men selected for their discretion, and their unwavering loyalty to the King. The hunting party travelled in boats, of which there were two, the King going in one, and his son Tŭngku Saleh in the other. In the latter boat sat Tûan Bângau, and about a dozen of the King's Youths. Arrived at a certain place, the King's boat went on round the point, and Tungku Saleh's boat tied up in mid-stream, while the Prince ate some sweatmeats which had been brought for the purpose.

When he had eaten his fill, he bade Tûan Bângau and one or two other Saiyids, who were among his followers, fall to on what remained, and it was while Tûan Bângau was washing his mouth over the side of the boat after eating, that Tûngku Saleh gave the signal which heralded his death. A man who was behind him stabbed him in the shoulder with a spear, and another blow given almost simultaneously knocked him into the river. Tûan Bângau dived, and swam until he had reached the shallow water near the bank. Here he rose to his feet, drew his *kris*, and called to those within the boat to come and fight him one at a time if they dared. The only answer was a spear which wounded him in the neck, and a bullet from a gun which penetrated to his heart. In a moment all that remained of Tûan Bângau was a shapeless heap of useless flesh, lying in the shallow water, with the eddies playing around and in and out of the brilliant silk garments, which had made him so brave a sight when alive. Those who had slain him, buried him; where, no man knoweth; the report that he had strayed and been lost, was diligently spread, and, though generally disbelieved, was found to be impossible of disproof. But Bêdah, his wife who had loved him, had learnt these things, and now told all to the White Man, hoping that thus her husband's murder might be avenged, and thereby she risked the life which his death had temporarily made desolate.

Compared with that of Âwang Îtam, however, Tûan Bângau's fate was a happy one. When the former disappeared from the sight of men, he was the victim of nameless tortures. As he told the tale of what he had suffered on the night that followed his arrest; of the ghastly tortures and mutilations which had wrecked his manhood, and left him the pitiable ruin he then was, the White Man writhed in sympathy, and was filled with a horror that made him sick.

'Better it were to die,' said he, 'than to live the life which is no life, and to suffer these nameless torments.'

'It is true,' said Âwang Îtam, 'it is true. But readily would I bear it over again, *Tûan*, if thereby for a little space I might be what I have been, and my Heart's Desire could once more be satisfied!'

These were the last words spoken while the dawn was breaking, as the White Man clambered over the side and wended his way homeward; and, therefore, I have called this tale the story of 'His Heart's Desire.'

A NIGHT OF TERROR

> The glaring eyes through the brushwood shine,
>   And the striped hide shows between
> The trees and bushes, 'mid trailing vine
>   And masses of ever-green.
> A snarling moan comes long and low,
>   We may neither flee nor fight,
> For well our leaping pulses know
>   The Terror that stalks by Night.

IF you put your finger on the map of the Malay Peninsula an inch or two from its exact centre, you will find a river in Pahang territory which has its rise in the watershed that divides that State from Kĕlantan and Trĕnggânu. This river is called the Tĕmbĕling, and it is chiefly remarkable for the number of its rapids and the richness of its gutta-bearing forests. Its inhabitants are a ruffianly lot of Malays, who are preyed upon by a family of *Wans*, a semi-royal set of nobles who do their best to live up to their traditions. Below the rapids the natives are chiefly noted for the quaint pottery that they produce from the clay which abounds there, and the rude shapes and ruder tracery of their vessels have probably suffered no change since the days when Solomon's fleets sought gold and peafowl and monkeys in the jungles of the Peninsula, as everybody knows. Above the rapids the Malays plant enough *gambir* to supply the wants of the whole betel-chewing population of Pahang, and, as the sale of this commodity wins them a few dollars annually, they are too indolent to plant their own rice. This grain, which is the staple of all Malays, without which they cannot live, is therefore sold to them by down river natives, at the exorbitant price of half a dollar the bushel.

A short distance up stream, and midway between the mouth and the big rapids, there is a straggling village, called Ranggul, the houses of which, made of wattled bamboos and thatched with palm leaves, stand on piles, amid the groves of cocoa-nut and areca-nut palms, varied by clumps of smooth-leaved banana trees. The houses are not very close together, but a man can call from one to the other with ease ; and thus the cocoa-nuts thrive, which, as the Malays say, grow not with pleasure beyond the sound of the human voice. The people of the village are not more indolent than other Malays. They plant a little rice, when the season comes, in the swamps behind the village. They work a little jungle produce, when the pinch of poverty drives them to it, but, like all Malays, they take life sufficiently easily. If you chance to go into the village of Ranggul, during any of the hot hours of the day, you will find most of its occupants lying about in their dark, cool houses, engaged upon such gentle mental tasks as may be afforded by whittling a stick, or hacking slowly at the already deeply scored threshold-block, with their clumsy wood-knives. Sitting thus, they gossip with a passing neighbour, who stops to chatter as he sits propped upon the stair ladder, or they croak snatches of song, with some old-world refrain to it, and, from time to time, break off to cast a word over their shoulders to the wife in the dim background near the fireplace, or to the little virgin daughter, carefully secreted on the shelf overhead, in company with a miscellaneous collection of dusty, grimy rubbish, the disused lumber of years. Nature has been very lavish to the Malay, and she has provided him with a soil which returns a maximum of food for a minimum of grudging labour. The cool, moist fruit groves call aloud to all mankind to come and revel in their fragrant shade during the parching hours of mid-day, and the Malay has caught the spirit of his surroundings, and is very much what Nature has seen fit to make him.

Some five-and-thirty years ago, when Che' Wan Âhmad, now better known as Sultân Âhmad Maätham Shah, was collecting his forces in Dûngun, preparatory to making his last and successful descent into the Tĕmbĕling valley, whence to overrun and conquer Pahang, the night was closing in at Ranggul. A large house stood, at that time, in a somewhat isolated position, within a thickly-planted compound, at one extremity of the village. In this house, on the night of which I write, seven men and two women were at work on the evening meal. The men sat in the centre of the floor, on a white mat made from the plaited leaves of the *mĕngkûang* palm, with a plate piled with rice before each of them, and a brass tray, holding various little china bowls of curry, placed where all could reach it. They sat cross-legged, with bowed backs, supporting themselves on their left arms, the left hand lying flat on the mat, and being so turned that the outspread fingers pointed inwards. With the fingers of their right hands they messed the rice, mixing the curry well into it, and then swiftly carried a large handful to their mouths, skilfully, without dropping a grain. The women sat demurely, in a half kneeling position, with their feet tucked away under them, and ministered to the wants of the men. They said never a word, save an occasional exclamation, when they drove away a lean cat that crept too near to the food, and the men also held their peace. There was no sound to be heard, save the hum of the insects out of doors, the deep note of the bull-frogs in the rice swamps, and the unnecessarily loud noise of mastication made by the men as they ate.

When the meal was over the women carried what was left to a corner near the fireplace, and there fell to on such of the viands as their lords had not consumed. If you had looked carefully, however, you would have seen that the cooking-pots, over which the women ruled, still held a secret store for their own consumption, and that the quality of the food in this *cache* was by no means inferior to that which had been allotted to the men. In a land where women wait upon themselves, and have none to attend to their wants, or forestall their wishes, they very soon acquire an extremely good notion of how to look after themselves; and, since they have never known a state of society in which women are treated as they are amongst ourselves, they do not repine, and seem, for the most part, to be sufficiently bright, light-hearted, and happy.

The men, meanwhile, had each rolled up a quid of betel-nut, taking the four ingredients carefully from the little brass boxes in the wooden tray before them, and having prepared cigarettes of Javenese tobacco, with the dried shoots of the *nîpah* palm for wrappers, had at length broken the absorbed silence, which had held them fast while the matter of the meal was occupying their undivided attention.

The talk flitted lightly over many subjects; for a hearty meal, and the peace of soul which repletion brings with it, are not conducive to concentration of attention, nor yet to activity of mind. The Malay, too, is always superficial, and talk among natives generally plays round facts, rather than round ideas. Che' Sĕman, the owner of the house, and his two sons, Âwang and Ngah, discussed the prospects of the crop then growing in the fields behind the compound. Their cousin Äbdollah, who chanced to be passing the night in the house, told of a fall which his wife's aunt's brother had come by, when climbing a cocoanut tree. Mat, his *biras* (for they had married two sisters, which established a definite form of relationship between them, according to Malay ideas), added a few more or less ugly details to Äbdollah's description of the corpse after the accident. And as this attracted the attention of the two remaining men, Pôtek and Kassim, who had been discussing the price of rice, and the varying chances of *gĕtah* hunting, the talk at this point became general. Pôtek and Kassim had recently returned from Dûngun, where, as has been said, the present Sultân of Pahang was, at that time, collecting the force with which he afterwards successfully invaded and conquered the State. They told of all they had seen and heard, multiplying their figures with the daring recklessness that is born of unfettered imaginations, and the lack of a rudimentary knowledge of arithmetic. But even this absorbing topic could not hold the attention of their hearers for long. Before Pôtek and Kassim had well finished the enumeration of the heavy artillery, of the thousands of the elephants, and the tens of thousands of the followers, with which they credited the adventurous, but slender bands of ragamuffins, who followed Âhmad's fortunes, Che' Sĕman broke into their talk with words on a subject which, at that time, was ever uppermost in the minds of the Tĕmbĕling people, and the conversation straightway drifted into the channel in which it had run, with only casual interruptions, for many weeks past.

'He of the Hairy Face[1] is with us once more,' ejaculated Che' Sĕman; and when this announcement had caused a dead silence to fall upon his hearers, and had even stilled the chatter of the women-folk near the fireplace, he continued:

'At the hour when the cicada is heard (sunset), I met Imâm Sîdik of Gĕmûroh, and bade him stay to eat rice, but he would not, saying that He of the Hairy Face had made his kill at Làbu yesternight, and it behoved all men to be within their houses before the darkness fell. And so saying he paddled his dug-out down stream with the short quick stroke used when we race boats. Imâm Sîdik is a wise man, and his words are true. He of the Hairy Face spares neither

---

[1] *Si Pûdong* = one of the names used by jungle-bred Malays to describe a tiger. They avoid using the beast's real name lest the sound of it should reach his ears, and cause him to come to the speaker.

priest nor prince. The girl he killed at Lâbu was a daughter of the *Wans*—her name Wan Ësah.'

'That makes three-and-twenty whom He of the Hairy Face hath slain in one year of maize' (three months), said Âwang in a low fear-stricken voice. 'He touches neither goats nor kine, and men say He sucketh more blood than He eateth flesh.'

'That it is which proves Him to be the thing he is,' said Ngah.

'Thy words are true,' said Che' Sĕman solemnly. 'He of the Hairy Face has his origin in a man. The *Sĕmang*—the negrits of the woods—drove him forth from among them, and now he lives solitarily in the jungles, and by night he takes upon himself the form of Him of the Hairy Face, and feasts upon the flesh of his own kind.'

'I have heard tell that it is only the men of Korinchi who have this strange power,' interposed Äbdollah, in the tone of one who longs to be reassured.

'Men say that they also possess the power,' rejoined Che' Sĕman, 'but certain it is that He of the Hairy Face was born a *Sĕmang*,—a negrit of the woods,—and when He goeth forth in human guise he is like all other *Sĕmangs* to look upon. I and many others have seen him, roaming alone, naked, and muttering to himself, when we have been in the forests seeking for jungle produce. All men know that it is He who by night harries us in our villages. If one ventures to go forth from our houses in the time of darkness, to the bathing raft at the river's edge, or to tend our sick, or to visit a friend, Si Pûdong is ever to be found watching, and thus the tale of his kills waxes longer and longer.'

'But men are safe from him while they sit within their houses?' asked Mat with evident anxiety.

'God alone knows,' answered Che' Sĕman piously, 'who can say where men are safe from Him of the Hairy Face? He cometh like a shadow, and slays like a prince, and then like a shadow he is gone! And the tale of his kills waxes ever longer and yet more long. May God send Him far from us! Ya Allah! It is He! Listen!'

At the word, a dead silence, broken only by the hard breathing of the men and women, fell upon all within the house. Then very faintly, and far away up stream, but not so faintly but that all could hear it, and shudder at the sound, the long-drawn, howling, snarling moan of a hungry tiger broke upon the stillness. The Malays call the roar of the tiger *äum*, and the word is vividly onomatopœtic, as those who have heard the sound in the jungle during the silent night watches can bear witness. All who have listened to the tiger in his forest freedom know that he has many voices wherewith to speak. He can give a barking cry, which is not unlike that of a deer; he can grunt like a startled boar, and squeak like the monkeys cowering at his approach in the branches overhead; he can shake the earth with a vibrating, resonant purr, like the sound of faint thunder in the foot-hills; he can mew and snarl like an angry wildcat; and he can roar like a lusty lion cub. But it is when he lifts up his voice in the long-drawn moan that the jungle chiefly fears him. This cry means that he is hungry, and, moreover, that he is so sure of his kill that he cares not if all the world knows that his belly is empty. It has something strangely horrible in its tone, for it speaks of that cold-blooded, dispassionate cruelty which is only to be found in perfection in the feline race. These sleek, smooth-skinned, soft-footed, lithe, almost serpentine animals, torture with a grace of movement, and a gentleness in strength which has something in it more violently repugnant to our natures than any sensation with which the thought of the blundering charge and savage goring of the buffalo, or the clumsy kneading with giant knee-caps, that the elephant metes out to its victims, can ever inspire in us.

Again the long-drawn moaning cry broke upon the stillness. The cattle in the byre heard it and were panic-stricken. Half mad with fear, they charged the walls of their pen, bearing all before them, and in a moment could be heard in the distance plunging madly through the brushwood, and splashing through the soft earth of the *pádi* fields. The dogs whimpered and scampered off in every direction, while the fowls beneath the house set up a drowsy and discordant screeching. The folk within the house were too terror-stricken to speak, for fear, which gives voices to the animal world, renders voluble human beings dumb. And all this time the cry broke forth again and again, ever louder and louder, as He of the Hairy Face drew nearer and yet more near.

At last the cruel whining howl sounded within the very compound in which the house stood, and its sudden proximity caused Mat to start so violently that he overturned the pitch torch at his elbow, and extinguished the flickering light. The women crowded up against the men, seeking comfort by physical contact with them, their teeth chattering like castanets. The men gripped their spears, and squatted tremblingly in the half light thrown by the dying embers of the fire, and the flecks cast upon floor and wall by the faint moonbeams struggling through the interstices of the thatched roof.

'Fear nothing, Mînah,' Che' Sĕman whispered, in a hoarse, strange voice, to his little daughter, who nestled miserably against his breast, 'in a space He will be gone. Even He of the Hairy Face will do us no harm while we sit within the house.'

Che' Sĕman spoke from the experience of many generations of Malays, but he knew not the nature of the strange beast with whom he had to deal. Once more the moan-like howl broke out on the still night air, but this time the note had changed, and gradually it quickened to the ferocious snarling roar, the charge song, as the tiger rushed forward and leaped against the side of the house with a heavy jarring thud. A shriek from all the seven throats went up on the instant, and then came a scratching, tearing sound, followed by a soft, dull flop, as the tiger, failing to effect a landing on the low roof, fell back to earth. The men started to their feet, clutching their weapons convulsively, and, led by Che' Sĕman, they raised, above the shrieks of the frightened women, a lamentable attempt at a *sôrak*, the Malayan war-cry, which is designed as much to put heart into those who utter it, as to frighten the enemy in defiance of whom it is sounded.

Mat, the man who had upset the torch and plunged the house in darkness, alone failed to add his voice to the miserable cheer raised by his fellows. Wild with fear of the beast without, he crept, unobserved by the others, up into the *pâra,* or shelf-like upper apartment, on which Mînah had been wont to sit, when strangers were about, during the short days of her virginity. This place, as is usual in most Malay houses, hardly deserved to be dignified by being termed a room. It consisted of a platform suspended from the roof in one corner of the house, and among the dusty lumber with which it was covered Mat now cowered and sought to hide himself.

A minute or two of sickening suspense followed the tiger's first unsuccessful charge. But presently the howl broke forth again, quickened rapidly to the note of the charge song, and once more the house trembled under the weight of the great animal. This time the leap of Him of the Hairy Face had been of truer aim, and a crash overhead, a shower of leaflets of thatch, and an ominous creaking of the woodwork told the cowering people in the house that their enemy had effected a landing on the roof.

The miserable thready cheer, which Che' Sĕman exhorted his fellows to raise in answer to the charge song of the tiger, died down in their throats. All looked upwards in deadly fascination as the thatch was torn violently apart by the great claws of their assailant. There were no firearms in the house, but the men instinctively grasped their spears, and held them ready to await the tiger's descent. Thus for a moment, as the quiet moonlight poured in through the gap in the thatch, they stood gazing at the great square face, marked with its black bars, at the flaming eyes, and the long cruel teeth framed in the hole which the claws of the beast had made. The timbers of the roof bent and cracked anew under the unwonted weight, and then, with the agility of a cat, He of the Hairy Face leaped lightly down, and was in among them before they knew. The striped hide was slightly wounded by the spears, but the shock of the brute's leap bore all who had resisted it to the floor. The tiger never stayed to use its jaws. It sat up, much in the attitude of a kitten which plays with something dangled before its eyes, and the soft pit-pat of its paws, as it struck out rapidly and with unerring aim, speedily disposed of all its enemies. Che' Sĕman, with his two sons, Âwang and Ngah, were the first to fall. Then Iang, Che' Sĕman's wife, reeled backwards against the wall, with her skull crushed out of all resemblance to any human member, by the awful strength of one of those well-aimed buffets from the fearful claws. Kassim, Pôtek, and Äbdollah fell before the tiger in quick succession, and Mînah, the girl who had nestled against her father for protection, lay now under his dead body, sorely wounded, wild with terror, but still alive and conscious. Mat, cowering on the shelf overhead, breathless with fear, and gazing fascinated at the carnage going on within a few feet of him, was the only inmate of the house who remained uninjured.

He of the Hairy Face killed quickly and silently, while there were yet some alive to resist him. Then, purring gently, he drank a deep draught of blood from each of his slaughtered victims. At last he reached Che' Sĕman, and Mînah, seeing him approach, made a feeble effort to evade him. Then began a fearful scene, the tiger playing with, and torturing the girl, just as we all have seen a cat do with a maimed mouse. Again and again Mînah crawled feebly away from her tormentor, only to be drawn back again just when escape seemed possible. Again and again she lay still in the utter inertia of exhaustion, only to be quickened into agonised movement once more by the touch of the tiger's cruel claws. Yet so cunningly did he play with her, that, as Mat described it, a time as long as it would take to cook rice had elapsed, before the girl was finally put out of her misery.

Even then He of the Hairy Face did not quit the scene of slaughter. Mat, as he lay trembling in the shelf overhead, watched the tiger, through the long hours of that fearful night, play with the mangled bodies of each of his victims in turn. He leaped from one to the other, inflicting a fresh blow with teeth or claws on their torn flesh, with all the airy, light-hearted agility and sinuous grace of a kitten playing with its shadow in the sun. Then when the dawn was breaking, the tiger tore down the door, leaped lightly to the ground, and betook himself to the jungle.

When the sun was up, an armed party of neighbours came to the house to see if ought could be done. But they found the place a shambles, the bodies hardly to be recognised, the floor-laths dripping blood, and Mat lying face downward on the shelf, with his reason tottering in the balance. The bodies, though they had been horribly mutilated, had not been eaten, the tiger having contented himself with drinking the blood of his victims, and playing his ghastly game with them till the dawn broke.

This is, I believe, the only recorded instance in the Peninsula of a tiger having dared to attack men within their closed houses; and the circumstances are so remarkable in every way, that I, for one, cannot find it in me to greatly blame the Malays for attributing the fearlessness of mankind, and the lust for blood displayed by Him of the Hairy Face, to the fact that he owed his existence to magic agencies, and was in reality no mere wild beast, but a member of the race upon which he so cruelly preyed.

IN THE DAYS WHEN THE LAND WAS FREE

> Alas, the shifting years have sped,
> Since we were hale and strong,
> Who oft have seen the hot blood shed,
> Nor held the deed a wrong;
> When the flames leap'd bright, thro' the frightened night,
> When the *sĕrak* rang thro' the lea,
> When a man might fight, and when might was right,
> In the Days when the Land was Free.
> *The Song of the Fettered Folk.*

IN 1873 the people of Pahang who, then as now, were ever ready to go upon the war-path, poured over the cool summits of the range that forms at once the backbone of the Peninsula and the boundary between Pahang and Sĕlângor. They went, at the invitation of the British Government, to bring to a final conclusion the protracted struggles, in which Malay *Rájas*, foreign mercenaries, and Chinese miners had alike been engaged for years, distracting the State of Sĕlângor, and breaking the peace of the Peninsula. A few months later, the Pahang Army, albeit sadly reduced by cholera, poured back again across the mountains, the survivors slapping their chests and their *kris*-hilts, and boasting loudly of their deeds, as befitted victorious warriors in a Malay land. The same stories are still told 'with circumstance and much embroidery,' by those who took part in the campaign, throughout the length and breadth of Pahang even unto this day.

Among the great Chiefs who led their people across the range, one of the last to go, and one of those whose heart was most uplifted by victory, was the present Mahràja Pĕrba of Jĕlai, commonly called To' Râja. His own people, even at that time, gave him the title he now bears, but the Bĕndăhàra of Pahang (since styled Sultân) had never formally installed him in the hereditary office of which he was the heir, so by the Court Faction he was still addressed as Pănglîma Prang Mâmat.

On his arrival at Pĕkan, the Pănglîma Prang, unmindful of the fate which, at an earlier period, had befallen his brother Wan Bong, whose severed head lay buried somewhere near the palace in a nameless grave, began to assert himself in a manner which no Malay King could be expected to tolerate. Not content with receiving from his own people the semi-royal honours, which successive To' Râjas have insisted upon from the natives of the interior, Pănglîma Prang allowed his pride to run away with both his prudence and his manners. He landed at Pĕkan with a following of nearly fifty men, all wearing shoes, the spoils of war, it is said, which had fallen to his lot through the capture of a Chinese store; he walked down the principal street of the town with an umbrella carried by one of his henchmen; and he ascended into the King's *Bâlai* with his *kris* uncovered by the folds of his *sârong!* The enormity of these proceedings may not, perhaps, be apparent; but, in those days, the wearing of shoes of a European type, and the public use of an umbrella, were among the proudest privileges of royalty. To ascend the *Bâlai* with an uncloaked weapon in one's girdle was, moreover, a warlike proceeding, which can only be compared to the snapping of fingers in the face of royalty. Therefore, when Pănglîma Prang left Pĕkan, and betook himself up river to his house in the Jĕlai, he left a flustered court, and a very angry King behind him.

But at this time there was a man in Pahang who was not slow to seize an opportunity, and in the King's anger he saw a chance that he had long been seeking. This man was Dàto' Imâm Prang Indĕra Gâjah Pahang, a title which, being interpreted, meaneth, The War Chief, the Elephant of Pahang. Magnificent and high sounding as was this name, it was found too large a mouthful for everyday use, and to the people of Pahang he was always known by the abbreviated title of To' Gâjah. He had risen from small beginnings by his genius for war, and more especially for that branch of the science which the Malays call *tîpu prang*—the deception of strife—a term which is more accurately rendered into English by the word treachery, than by that more dignified epithet strategy. He had already been the recipient of various land grants from the King, which carried with them some hundreds of devoted families who chanced to live on the alienated territories; he already took rank as a great Chief; but his ambition was to become the master of the Lĭpis Valley, in which he had been born, by displacing the aged To' Kâya Stiawangsa, the hereditary Chief of the District.

To' Gâjah knew that To' Kâya of Lĭpis, and all his people were more or less closely related to Pănglima Prang, and to the Jĕlai natives. He foresaw that, if war was declared against Pănglîma Prang by the King, the Lĭpis people would throw in their fortunes with the former. It was here, therefore, that he saw his chance, and, as the fates would have it, an instrument lay ready to his hand.

At Kuâla Lĭpis there dwelt in those days an old and cross-grained madman, a Jĕlai native by birth, who, in the days before his trouble came upon him, had been a great Chief in Pahang. He bore the title of Ôrang Kâya Haji, and his eldest son was named Wan Lingga. The latter was as wax in To' Gâjah's hands, and when they had arranged between themselves that in the event of a campaign against Pănglîma Prang proving successful, Wan Lingga should replace the latter by becoming To' Râja of Jĕlai, while the Lĭpis Valley should be allotted to To' Gâjah, with the title of Dâto' Kâya Stia-wangsa, they together approached the Bĕndăhâra on the subject.

They found him willing enough to entertain any scheme, which included the humbling of his proud vassal Pănglîma Prang, who so lately had done him dishonour in his own capital. Moreover the Bĕndăhâra of Pahang was as astute as it is given to most men to be, and he saw that strife between the great Chiefs mùst, by weakening all, eventually strengthen his own hand, since he would, in the end, be the peacemaker between them. Therefore he granted a letter of authority to Wan Lingga and To' Gâjah, and thus the war began.

The people of Pahang flocked to the interior, all noisily eager to stamp out of existence the upstart Chief, who had dared to wear shoes, and to carry an umbrella in the streets of their King's capital. The aged Chief of Lĭpis and his people, however, clove to Pănglîma Prang, or To' Râja, as he now openly called himself, and the war did not prosper. To' Gâjah had inspired but little love in the hearts of the men whom the Bĕndăhâra had given him for a following, and they allowed their stockades to be taken without a blow by the Jĕlai people, and on one occasion To' Gâjah only escaped by being paddled hastily down stream concealed in the rolled up hide of a buffalo.

At last it became evident that war alone could never subdue the Jĕlai and Lĭpis districts, and consequently negotiations were opened. A Chief named the Orang Kâya Pahlâwan of Sĕmantan visited To' Râja in the Jĕlai, and besought him to make his peace by coming to Pĕkan.

'Thou hast been victorious until now,' said he, 'but thy food is running low. How then wilt thou fare? It were better to submit to the Bĕndăhâra, and I will go warrant that no harm befalls thee. If the Bĕndăhâra shears off thy head, he shall only do so when thy neck has been used as a block for mine own. And thou knowest that the King loveth me.' To' Râja therefore allowed himself to be persuaded, but stipulated that Wan Lingga, who was then at Kuâla Lĭpis, should also go down to Pĕkan, since if he remained in the interior he might succeed in subverting the loyalty of the Jĕlai people who hitherto had been faithful to To' Râja. Accordingly Wan Lingga left Kuâla Lĭpis, ostensibly for Pĕkan, but, after descending the river for a few miles, he turned off into a side stream, named the Kĭchan, where he lay hidden biding his time.

When To' Râja heard of this, he at first declined to continue his journey down stream, but at length, making a virtue of necessity, he again set forward, saying that he entertained no fear of Wan Lingga, since one who could hide in the forest 'like a fawn or a mouse-deer' could never, he said, fill the seat of To' Râja of Jĕlai.

It is whispered, that it had been To' Gâjah's intention to make away with To' Râja, on his way down stream, by means of that 'warlike' art for which, I have said, he had a special aptitude; but the Jĕlai people knew the particular turn of the genius with which they had to deal, and consequently they remained very much on their guard. They travelled, some forty or fifty strong, on an enormous bamboo raft, with a large fortified house erected in its centre. They never parted with their arms, taking them both to bed and to bath; they turned out in force at the very faintest alarm of danger; they moored the raft in mid-stream when the evening fell; and, wonderful to relate, for Malays make bad sentinels, they kept faithful watch both by day and by night. Thus at length they won to Pĕkan without mishap; and thereafter they were suffered to remain in peace, no further and immediate attempts being made upon their lives.

To' Râja—or Pănglîma Prang as he was still called by the King and the Court Faction—remained at the capital a prisoner in all but the name. The Běndăhâra declined to accord him an interview, pointedly avoided speech with him, when they chanced to meet in public, and resolutely declined to allow him to leave Pěkan. This, in ancient days, was practically the King's only means of punishing a powerful vassal, against whom he did not deem it prudent to take more active measures; and as, at a Malay Court, the *entourage* of the Râja slavishly follow any example which their King may set them, the position of a great Chief living at the capital in disgrace was sufficiently isolated, dreary, humiliating, and galling.

But To' Râja's own followers clove to him with the loyalty for which, on occasion, the natives of Pahang are remarkable. The Běndăhâra spared no pains to seduce them from their allegiance, and the three principal Chieftains who followed in To' Râja's train were constantly called into the King's presence, and were shown other acts of favour, which were steadfastly denied to their master. But it profited the Běndăhâra nothing, for Imâm Bakar, the oldest of the three, set an example of loyalty which his two companions, Imâm Prang Sâmah and Khatib Bûjang, followed resolutely. Imâm Bakar himself acted from principle. He was a man whom Nature had endowed with firm nerves, a faithful heart, and that touch of recklessness and fatalism which is needed to put the finishing touch to the courage of an oriental. He loved To' Râja and all his house, nor could he be tempted or scared into a denial of his affection and loyalty. Imâm Prang Sàmah and Khatib Bûjang, both of whom I know well, are men of a different type. They belong to the weak-kneed brethren, and they followed Imâm Bakar because they feared him and To' Râja. They found themselves, to use an emphatic colloquialism, between the Devil and the Deep Sea, nor had they sufficient originality between them to suggest a compromise. Thus they imitated Imâm Bakar, repeated his phrases after him, and, in the end, but narrowly escaped sharing with him the fate which awaits those who arouse the wrath of a King.

At each interview which these Chieftains had with their monarch, the latter invariably concluded the conversation by calling upon them to testify to the faith that was in them.

'Who,' he would ask, 'is your Master, and who is your Chief?'

And the three, led by Imâm Bakar, would make answer with equal regularity:

'Thou, O Highness, art Master of thy servants, and His Highness To' Râja is thy servants' Chief.'

Now, from the point of view of the Bĕndâhâra, this answer was most foully treasonable. That in speaking to him, the King, they should give To' Râja—the vassal he had been at such pains to humble—a royal title equal to his own, was in itself bad enough. But that, not content with this outrage, they should decline to acknowledge the Bĕndâhâra as both Master and Chief was the sorest offence of all. A man may own duty to any Chief he pleases, until such time as he comes into the presence of his King, who is the Chief of Chiefs. Then all loyalty to minor personages must be laid aside, and the Monarch must be acknowledged as the Master and Lord above all others. But it was just this one thing that Imâm Bakar was determined not to do, and at each succeeding interview the anger of the Bĕndăhâra waxed hotter and hotter.

At the last interview of all, and before the fatal question had been asked and answered, the King spoke with the three Chieftains concerning the manner of their life in the remote interior, and, turning to Imâm Bakar, he asked how they of the upper country lived.

'Thy servants live on earth,' replied the Imâm, meaning thereby that they were tillers of the soil.

When they had once more given the hateful answer to the oft put question, and had withdrawn in fear and trembling before the King's anger, the latter called To' Gâjah to him and said :

'Imâm Bakar and the men his friends told me a moment since that they eat earth. Verily the Earth will have its revenge, for I foresee that in a little space the Earth will swallow Imâm Bakar.'

Next day the three recalcitrant Chiefs left Pĕkan for their homes in the interior, and, a day or two later, To' Gâjah, by the Bĕndăhâra's order, followed them in pursuit. His instructions were to kill all three without further questionings, should he chance to overtake them before they reached their homes at Kuâla Tĕmbĕling. If, however, they should win to their homes in safety, they were once more to be asked the fatal question, and their lives were to depend upon the nature of their answer. This was done, lest a rising of the Chieftains' relations should give needless trouble to the King's people; for the clan was not a small one, and any unprovoked attack upon the villages, in which the Chieftains lived, would be calculated to give offence.

Imâm Bakar and his friends were punted up the long reaches of the Pahang river, past the middle country, where the banks are lined with villages nestling in the palm and fruit trees; past Gûnong Sĕnuyum—the Smiling Mountain—that great limestone rock, which raises its crest high above the forest that clothes the plain in which it stands in solitary beauty; past Lûbok Plang, where in a nameless grave lies the Princess of ancient story, the legend of whose loveliness alone survives; past Glanggi's Fort, those gigantic caves which seem to lend some probability to the tradition that, before they changed to stone, they were once the palace of a King; and on and on, until, at last, the yellow sandbanks of Pâsir Tambang came in sight. And close at their heels, though they knew it not, followed To' Gâjah and those of the King's Youths who had been deputed to cover their Master's shame.

At Kuâla Tĕmbĕling, where the waters of the river of that name make common cause with those of the Jĕlai, and where the united streams first take the name of Pahang, there lies a broad stretch of sand glistening in the fierce sunlight. It has been heaped up, during countless generations, by little tributes from the streams which meet at its feet, and it is never still. Every flood increases or diminishes its size, and weaves its restless sands into some new fantastic curve or billow. The sun which beats upon it bakes the sand almost to boiling point, and the heat-haze dances above it, like some restless phantom above a grave. And who shall say that ghosts of the dead and gone do not haunt this sandbank far away in the heart of the Peninsula? If native report speaks true, the spot is haunted, for the sand, they say, is 'hard ground' such as the devils love to dwell upon. Full well may it be so, for Pâsir Tambang has been the scene of many a cruel tragedy, and could its sands but speak, what tales would they have to tell us of woe and murder, of valour and treachery, of shrieking souls torn before their time from their sheaths of flesh and blood, and of all the savage deeds of this

> race of venomous worms
> That sting each other here in the dust.

It was on this sandbank that To' Gâjah and his people pitched their camp, building a small open house with rude uprights, and thatching it with palm leaves cut in the neighbouring jungle. To' Gâjah knew that Imâm Bakar was the man with whom he really had to deal. Imâm Prang Sâmah and Khatib Bûjang he rated at their proper worth, and it was to Imâm Bakar, therefore, that he first sent a message, desiring him once more to answer as to who was his Master and who his Chief. Imâm Bakar, after consulting his two friends, once more returned the answer that while he acknowledged the Běndähâra as his King and his Master, his immediate Chief was no other than 'His Highness To' Râja.' That answer sealed his doom.

On the following day To' Gàjah sent for Imàm Bakar, and made all things ready against his coming. To this end he buried his spears and other arms under the sand within his hut.

When the summons to visit To' Gâjah reached Imâm Bakar, he feared that his time had come. He was not a man, however, who would willingly fly from danger, and he foresaw moreover that if he took refuge in flight all his possessions would be destroyed by his enemies, while he himself, with his wife and little ones, would die in the jungles or fall into the hands of his pursuers. He already regarded himself as a dead man, but though he knew that he could save himself even now by a tardy desertion of To' Râja, the idea of adopting this means of escape was never entertained by him for an instant.

'If I sit down, I die, and if I stand up, I die!' he said to the messenger. 'Better then does it befit a man to die standing. Come, let us go to Pâsir Tambang and learn what To' Gâjah hath in store for me!'

The sun was half-mast high in the heavens as Imâm Bakar crossed the river to Pâsir Tambang in his tiny dug-out. Until the sun's rays fall more or less perpendicularly, the slanting light paints broad reaches of water a brilliant dazzling white, unrelieved by shadow or reflection. The green of the masses of jungle on the river banks takes to itself a paler hue than usual, and the yellow of the sandbanks changes its shade from the colour of a cowslip to that of a pale and early primrose. It was on such a white morning as this that Imâm Bakar crossed slowly to meet his fate. His dug-out grounded on the sandbank, and when it had been made fast to a pole, its owner, fully armed, walked towards the hut in which To' Gâjah was seated.

This Chief was a very heavily built man, with a bullet-shaped head, and a square resolute jaw, partially cloaked by a short sparse beard of coarse wiry hair. His voice and his laugh were both loud and boisterous, and he usually affected an air of open, noisy good-fellowship, which was but little in keeping with his character. When he saw Imâm Bakar approaching him, with the slow and solemn tread of one who believes himself to be walking to his death, he cried out to him, while he was yet some way off, with every appearance of friendship and cordiality :

'O Imâm Bakar! What is the news? Come hither to me and fear nothing. I come as thy friend, in peace and love. Come let us touch hands in salutation as befits those who harbour no evil one to another.'

Imâm Bakar was astonished at this reception. His heart bounded against his ribs with relief at finding his worst fears so speedily dispelled, and being, for the moment, off his guard, he placed his two hands between those of To' Gâjah in the usual manner of Malay formal salutation. Quick as thought, To' Gâjah seized him by the wrists, his whole demeanour changing in a moment from that of the rough good-fellowship of the boon companion, to excited and cruel ferocity.

'Stab! Stab! Stab! Ye sons of evil women!' he yelled to his men, and before poor Imâm Bakar could free himself from the powerful grasp which held him, the spears were unearthed, and half a dozen of their blades met in his shuddering flesh. It was soon over, and Imâm Bakar lay dead upon the sandbank, his body still quivering, while the peaceful morning song of the birds came uninterrupted from the forest around.

Then Khatib Bûjang and Imâm Prang Sâmah were sent for, and as they came trembling into the presence of To' Gâjah, whose hands were still red with the blood of their friend and kinsman, they squatted humbly on the sand at his feet.

'Behold a sample of what ye also may soon be,' said To' Gâjah, spurning the dead body of Imâm Bakar as he spoke. 'Mark it well, and then tell me who is your Master and who your Chief!'

Khatib Bûjang and Imâm Prang Sâmah stuttered and stammered, but not because they hesitated about the answer, but rather through over eagerness to speak, and a deadly fear which held them dumb. At last, however, they found words and cried together:

'The Běndăhâra is our Master, and our Chief is whomsoever thou mayest be pleased to appoint.'

Thus they saved their lives, and are still living, while To' Gâjah lies buried in an exile's grave; but many will agree in thinking that such a death as Imâm Bakar's is a better thing for a man to win, than empty years such as his companions have survived to pass in scorn and in dishonour.

But while these things were being done at Pěkan and at Pâsir Tambang, Wan Lingga, who, as I have related, had remained behind in the upper country when To' Râja was carried to Pěkan, was sparing no pains to seduce the faithful natives of the interior from their loyalty to their hereditary Chief. In all his efforts, however, he was uniformly unsuccessful, for, though he had got rid of To' Râja, there remained in the Lĭpis Valley the aged Chief of the District, the Dâto' Kâya Stia-wangsa, whom the people both loved and feared. He had been a great warrior in the days of his youth, and a series of lucky chances and hair-breadth escapes had won for him an almost fabulous reputation, such as among a superstitious people easily attaches itself to any striking and successful personality. It was reported that he bore a charmed life, that he was invulnerable alike to lead bullets and to steel blades, and even the silver slugs which his enemies had fashioned for him had hitherto failed to find their billet in his body. From the first this man had thrown in his lot with his kinsman To' Râja, and, unlike him, he had declined to allow himself to be persuaded to visit the capital when the war came to an end. Thus he continues to live at the curious little village of Pĕnjum, on the Lĭpis river, and, so long as he was present in person to exert his influence upon the people, Wan Lingga found it impossible to make any headway against him.

These things were reported by Wan Lingga to To' Gâjah, and by the latter to the Bĕndăhâra. The result was an order to Wan Lingga, charging him to attack To' Kâya Stia-wangsa by night, and to slay him and all his house. With To' Kâya dead and buried, and To' Râja a State prisoner at the capital, the game which To' Gâjah and Wan Lingga had been playing would at least be won. The Lĭpis would fall to the former, and the Jĕlai to the latter as their spoils of war ; and the people of these Districts, being left 'like little chicks without the mother hen,' would acquiesce in the arrangement, following their new Chiefs as captives of their bows and spears.

Thus all looked well for the future when Wan Lingga set out, just before sun-down, from his house at Âtok to attack To' Kâya Stia-wangsa at Pĕnjum. The latter village was at that time inhabited by more Chinese than Malays. It was the nearest point on the river to the gold mines of Jâlis, and at the back of the squalid native shops, that lined the river bank, a well-worn footpath led inland to the Chinese alluvial washings. Almost in the centre of the long line of shops and hovels which formed the village of Pĕnjum, stood the thatched house in which To' Kâya Stia-wangsa lived, with forty or fifty women, and about a dozen male followers. The house was roofed with thatch. Its walls were fashioned from plaited laths of split bamboo, and it was surrounded by a high fence of the same material. This was the place which was to be Wan Lingga's object of attack.

A band of nearly a hundred men followed Wan Lingga from Âtok. Their way lay through a broad belt of virgin forest, which stretches between Âtok and Pĕnjum, a distance of about half a dozen miles. The tramp of the men moving in a single file through the jungle, along the narrow footpath, worn smooth by the passage of countless naked feet, made sufficient noise to scare all living things from their path. The forests of the Peninsula, even at night, when their denizens are afoot, are not cheerful places. Though a man lie very still, so that the life of the jungle is undisturbed by his presence, the weird night noises, that are borne to his ears, only serve to emphasise the solitude and the gloom. The white moonlight struggles in patches through the thick canopy of leaves overhead, and makes the shadows blacker and more awful by the contrast of light and shade. But a night march through the forest is even more depressing, when the soft pat of bare feet, the snapping of a dry twig, a whispered word of warning or advice, the dull deep note of the night-jar, and the ticking of the tree insects alone break the stillness. Nerves become strung to a pitch of intensity which the circumstances hardly seem to warrant, and all the chances of evil, which in the broad light of day a man would laugh to scorn, assume in one's mind the aspect of inevitable certainties.

I speak by the book; for well I know the depression, and the fearful presentiment of coming evil, which these night marches are apt to occasion; and well can I picture the feelings and thoughts which must have weighed upon Wan Lingga, during that four hours' silent tramp through the forest.

He was playing his last card. If he succeeded in falling upon To' Kâya unawares, and slaying him on the spot, all that he had longed for and dreamed of, all that he desired for himself and for those whom he held dear, all that he deemed to be of any worth, would be his for all his years. And if he failed?— He dared not think of what his position would then be; and yet it was this very thought that clung to him with such persistence during the slow march. He saw himself hated and abhorred by the people of the interior, who would then no longer have reason to fear him; he saw himself deserted by To' Gâjah, in whose eyes, he was well aware, he was merely regarded as a tool, to be laid aside when use for it was over ; he saw himself in disgrace with the King, whose orders he had failed to carry out ; and he saw himself a laughing stock in the land, one who had aspired and had not attained, one who had striven and had failed, with that grim phantom of hereditary madness, of which he was always conscious, stretching out its hand to seize him. All these things he saw and feared, and his soul sank within him.

At last Pĕnjum was reached, and To' Kâya's house was ringed about by Wan Lingga's men. The placid moonlight fell gently on the sleeping village, and showed Wan Lingga's face white with eagerness and anxiety, as he gave the word to fire. In a moment all was noise and tumult. Wan Lingga's men raised their war-yell, and shrieking ' By order of the King ! ' fired into To' Kâya's house. Old To' Kâya, thus rudely awakened, set his men to hold the enemy in check, and himself passed out of the house in the centre of the mob of his frightened women-folk. He was not seen until he reached the river bank, when he leaped into the stream, and, old man that he was, swam stoutly for the far side. Shot after shot was fired at him, and eight of them, it is said, struck him, though none of them broke the skin, and he won to the far side in safety. Here he stood for a moment, in spite of the hail of bullets with which his enemy greeted his landing. He shook his angry old arm at Wan Lingga, shouted a withering curse, took one sad look at his blazing roof-tree, and then plunged into the forest.

When the looting was over, Wan Lingga's people dispersed in all directions. Nothing, they knew, fails like failure, and the Lĭpis people, who would have feared to avenge the outrage had Wan Lingga been successful, would now, they feared, wreak summary punishment on those who had dared to attack their Chief. Wan Lingga, finding himself deserted, fled down stream, there to suffer all that he had foreseen and dreaded during that march through the silent forests. His mind gave way under the strain put upon it by the misery of his position at Pĕkan. The man who had failed was discredited and alone. His former friends stood aloof, his enemies multiplied exceedingly. So when the madness, which was in his blood, fell upon him at Pĕkan, he was thrust into a wooden cage, where he languished for years, tended as befits the madman whom the Malay ranks with the beasts.

When he regained his reason, the politics of the country had undergone a change, and his old ambitious dreams had faded away for ever. His old enemy To' Râja, whom he had sought to displace, was now ruling the Jĕlai, and enjoying every mark of the King's favour. Domestic troubles in the royal household had led the King to regard the friendship of this Chief as a matter of some importance, and Wan Lingga's chances of preferment were dead and buried.

He returned to his house at Âtok, where he lived, discredited and unhonoured, the object of constant slights. He spent his days in futile intrigues and plots, which were too impotent to be regarded seriously, or as anything but subjects for mirth, and, from time to time, his madness fell upon him, and drove him forth to wallow with the kine, and to herd with the beasts in the forest.

At last, in 1891, he resolved to put away the things of this world, and set out on the pilgrimage to Mecca. All was ready for his departure on the morrow, and his brethren crowded the little house at Âtok to wish him god-speed. But in the night the madness fell upon him once more, and rising up he ran *âmok* through his dwelling, slaying his wife and child, and wounding one of his brothers. Then he fled into the forest, and after many days was found hanging dead in the fork of a fruit-tree. He had climbed into the branches to sleep, and in his slumbers had slipped down into the fork where he had become tightly wedged. With his impotent arms hanging on one side of the tree, and his legs dangling limply on the other, he had died of exhaustion, alone and untended, without even a rag to cover his nakedness.

It was a miserable, and withal a tragic death, but not ill fitted to one who had staked everything to gain a prize he had not the strength to seize; one whom Fate had doomed to perpetual and inglorious failure.

UN MAUVAIS QUART D'HEURE

> Ere the moon has climbed the mountain, ere the rocks are ribbed with light,
> When the downward-dipping tails are dank and drear,
> Comes a breathing hard behind thee, *snuffle-snuffle* through the night—
> It is Fear, O Little Hunter, it is Fear!
> On thy knees and draw the bow; bid the shrilling arrow go;
> In the empty mocking thicket plunge the spear;
> But thy hands are loosed and weak, and the blood has left thy cheek—
> It is Fear, O Little Hunter, it is Fear!
>
> RUDYARD KIPLING's *Song of the Little Hunter*.

WE had been sitting late in the verandah of my bungalow of Kuâla Lĭpis, which overlooks the long and narrow reach, formed by the combined waters of the Lĭpis and the Jĕlai. The moon had risen some hours earlier, and the river ran white between the dark banks of jungle which seemed to fence it in on all sides. The ill-kept garden, with the tennis-ground, that never got beyond the stage of being dug up, and the rank grass behind the bamboo fence, were flooded with the soft light, every tattered detail of its ugliness showing as clearly as though it was noon. The night was very still, and the soft, scented air blew coolly round our faces.

I had been holding forth, to the handful of men who had been dining with me, on Malay beliefs and superstitions, while they manfully stifled their yawns. When a man has a smattering knowledge of anything, which is not usually known to his neighbours, it is a temptation to lecture on the subject, and, looking back, I fear that I had been on the rostrum during the best part of that evening. I had told them of the *Pĕnangal*, that horrible wraith of a woman who has died in child-birth, and who comes to torment small children, in the guise of a fearful face and bust, with many feet of bloody trailing entrails flying in her wake; of that weird little white animal the *Mati-ânak*, that makes beast noises round the graves of children; and of the familiar spirits that men raise up from the corpses of babes who have never seen the light, the tips of whose tongues they bite off and swallow, after the child has been brought back to life by magic agencies. It was at this point that young Middleton began to cock up his ears, and I, finding that one of my listeners was at last inclined to show some interest, launched out with renewed vigour, until my sorely tried companions had, one by one, gone off to bed, each to his own quarters.

Middleton was staying with me at the time, and he and I sat in silence looking at the light upon the river, and each thinking his own thoughts. Middleton was the first to speak.

'That was a curious myth you were telling us, about the *Pôlong*, the Familiar Spirits,' he said. 'I have heard of it before from natives, but there is a thing I have never spoken of, and always swore that I would keep to myself, that I have a good mind to tell you now, if you will promise not to call me a liar.'

'That is all right,' said I. 'Fire away.'

'Well,' said Middleton, puffing at his pipe, 'you remember Juggins, of course? He was a naturalist, you know, and he came to stay with me during the close season [1] last year. He was hunting for bugs and that sort of thing, and he used to fill my bungalow with all sorts of rotting green stuff, that he brought in from the jungle. He stopped with me for about ten days, and when he heard that I was bound for a trip up into the Sâkai country, he said he would come too. I did not mind much, as he was a decent beggar enough, in spite of his dirty ways, so I said all right, and we started up together. When we got well up into the Sâkai country, we had to leave our boats behind at the foot of the rapids, and leg it for the rest of the time. We had not enough bearers with us to take any food, and we lived pretty well on what we could get, yams, and tapioca, and Indian corn, and soft stuff of that sort. It was new to Juggins, and it used to give him awful gripes, but he stuck to it like a man.

'Well, one evening, when the night was shutting down pretty fast, Juggins and I got to a fairly large camp of Sâkai in the middle of a clearing, and of course all the beggars bolted into the jungle when we approached. We went on up to the largest hut of the lot, and there we found a woman lying by the side of her dead child. It was as stiff as Herod, though it had not been born more than half an hour, I should say, and I went up

---

[1] Close season = From November to February, when the rivers on the East Coast are closed to traffic by the North-East Monsoon.

into the house thinking I might be able to do something for the poor, wretched mother. She did not seem to see it, however, for she bit and snarled at me like a wounded animal, so I let her be, and Juggins and I took up our quarters in a smaller hut near by, which seemed fairly new, and was not so filthy dirty as most Sâkai lairs.

'Presently, when the beggars who had run away found out who it was, they began to come back again. You know their way. First a couple of men came and looked at us. Then I gave them some baccy, and spoke a word or two to them in *Sĕ-noi*, that always reassures them. Then they went back and fetched the others, and presently we were as comfortable as possible, though we *had* a dozen Sâkai to share our hut with us. Juggins complained awfully about the uneven flooring of boughs, which you know is pretty hard lying, and makes one's bones ache as though they were coming out at the joints, but we had had a tough day of it and I slept in spite of our hosts. I wonder why it is that Sâkai never sleep the whole night through like Christians. I suppose it is their animal nature, and that, like the beasts, they are most awake by night. You know how they lie about in the warm ashes of the fireplaces till they are black as sweeps, and then *how* they jabber. It is always a marvel to me what they find to yarn about. Even we white men run short of our stock of small-talk unless something happens to keep things going, or unless we have a beggar like you to jaw to us. They say that Englishmen talk about their tubs, when they run dry on all other subjects of conversation, but the Sâkai cannot talk about washing, for they never bathe by any chance, it makes that filthy skin disease they are covered with itch so awfully. It had rained a bit that night, when they were hiding away in the jungle, and I could hear their nails going on their dirty hides whenever I woke, and Juggins told me afterwards that they kept him awake by their jabber, and that each time he thought they had settled down for the night, he was disgusted to find that it was only another false start. Juggins tried to get a specimen of the bacillus that causes the skin disease, but I don't know whether he succeeded. I fancy it is due to want of blood. The poor brutes have never had enough to eat for a couple of hundred generations, and what food they do get is bloating beastly stuff. They do not get enough salt either, and that generally leads to skin disease. I have seen little brats, hardly able to stand, covered with it, the skin peeling off in flakes, and I used to frighten Juggins out of his senses by telling him that he had caught it, when his nose peeled with the sun.

'Well, in the morning we got up just in time to see the poor little dead baby, that I told you about, put into a hole in the ground. They fitted it into a piece of bark, and stuck it in the grave they had made for it on the edge of the clearing, and they put a flint and steel, and a wood-knife, and some food and things in with it, though no living baby could have had any use for half of them, let alone a dead one. Then the old medicine man of the tribe recited the ritual over the grave. I took the trouble to translate it once. It goes something like this:—

'"O Thou who hast gone forth from among those

who dwell upon the surface of the earth, and hast taken for thy dwelling-place the land which is beneath the earth! Fire have we given thee to light thy fires, raiment wherewith thou mayest be clothed, food to fill thy belly, and a knife to clear thy way. Go then and make unto thyself friends among those who dwell beneath the earth, and come back no more to trouble or molest those who live upon the earth's surface."

'It was short and sweet, and then they stamped down the soil, while the mother whimpered about the place like a cat that has lost its kittens. A mangy, half starved dog came and smelt hungrily about the grave, until it was sent howling away by a kick from one of the human animals near it; and a poor little brat, who set up a piping song, a few minutes later, was kicked, and cuffed, and knocked about, by every one who could reach him, with hand, foot, or missile. The Sâkai think it unlucky to sing or dance for nine days after a death, so the tribesmen had to give the poor little urchin, who had done the wrong, a fairly bad time of it to propitiate the dead baby.

'Then they began to pack up all their household gods, and in about an hour the last of the laden women, who was carrying so many babies, and cooking pots, and rattan bags and things, that she looked like the outside of a gipsy's cart at home, had filed out of the clearing, and Juggins and I, with our three or four Malays, were left in possession. The Sâkai always shift camp like that when a death occurs, because they think the ghost haunts the place where the body died, though what particular harm the ghost of a mite of a baby could do, I cannot pretend to say. When there is an epidemic among the Sâkai, they are so busy shifting camp, and building new huts, that they have not time to get proper food, and half those who do not die of the disease die of semi-starvation. They are a queer lot.

'Well,' continued young Middleton, whose pipe had gone out, and who was fairly into his stride now, 'Well, Juggins and I were left alone, and all that day we hunted through the jungle to try and get a shot at a *sĕlâdang*,[1] but we saw nothing, and we came back to the empty Sâkai camp at night, my Malays fairly staggering under the weight of the rubbish that Juggins used to call his botanical specimens. We got a meal of sorts, and I was lying off smoking, and thinking how lucky it was that the Sâkai had cleared out, when suddenly old Juggins sat up with his eyes fairly snapping at me.

'"I say," he said, "I must have that baby. It would make a ripping specimen."

'"It would make a ripping stink," I answered. "Go to sleep, Juggins, old man, the tapioca has gone to your head."

'"No, but I am serious," said Juggins, "I mean to have that baby whether you like it or no, and that is flat."

'"Yes," said I, "that is flat enough in all conscience, but I wish you would give it up. People do not like having their dead tampered with."

'"No," said Juggins again, rising as he spoke, and reaching for his shoes, "No, I am going to dig it up now."

'"Juggins," said I sharply, "sit down! You are

[1] *Sĕlâdang* = wild buffalo.

a lunatic of course, but I was another to bring you up here with me, knowing as I did the particular species of crank you are; and if you really are set on this beastly thing, I suppose I must not leave you in the lurch; though upon my word I do *not* like the notion of turning resurrection man in my old age."

' "You are a brick!" cried Juggins, jumping up again and fumbling at his boot laces, "Come along!"

' "Sit down, man!" said I in a tone which cooled his enthusiasm for the moment. "I have said that I will see you through, and that is enough. But mind this, you have to do what I tell you. I know more about the people and the country than you do, and I am not going to lose caste with my Malays, and perhaps get stranded in this god-forsaken jumping-off place, just because you choose to do a fool's deed in a fool's own way. These Malays of mine here have no particular love for the exhumed bodies of dead babies, and they would not understand what any sane man could want fooling about with such a thing. They have not been educated up to that pitch of interest in the secrets of science which seems to have made a lunatic of you. If they could understand what we are saying now, they would think that you wanted the kid's body for some devilry or witchcraft business, and we should as like as not get left by them. Then who would carry your precious specimens back to the boats? I would not lift a finger to help you, and I am not over sure that I could even guide you back, if it came to that. No, this thing cannot be done until my people are all asleep, so lie still and wait till I give you the word."

'Juggins groaned, and tried to persuade me to let him go at once, but I replied that nothing would induce me to go before one o'clock, and, so saying, I turned over on my side, and lay reading and smoking, while Juggins fumed and fretted, as he watched the slow hands creeping round the dial of his watch.

'I always take books with me, as you know, when I go into the jungle, and I remember that that evening I lay reading Miss Florence Montgomery's *Misunderstood*, with the tears running down my nose. When at last Juggins whispered that time was up, that pretty story of child life had made me more sick with Juggins and his disgusting scheme than ever.

'I never felt so like a criminal in all my life as I did that night as Juggins and I crept out of the hut, over the sleeping bodies of my Malays; nor did I know before, how hard it is to walk on an openwork flooring of sticks and boughs, if one is anxious to do it without making a noise. We got out of the house at last, without waking any of my fellows, and then began to creep along the edge of the jungle that lined the clearing. Why did we think it necessary to creep? I do not know, but somehow the long wait, and the uncanny sort of work we were after, had set our nerves going a bit. The night was as still as most nights are in real *pukka* jungle, that is to say it was as full of noises—little quiet beast and tree noises—as an egg's full of meat, and every one of them made me jump like a half broken gee shying. There was not a breath of air blowing in the clearing, but the clouds were racing across the moon miles up above our heads, and the moon looked as though it was scudding through them in the opposite direction like a great white fire balloon. It was dark along the edge of the clearing, for the jungle threw a heavy shadow, and Juggins kept knocking those great clumsy feet of his against the stumps, and swearing softly, under his breath.

'When we got near the grave, the moon came out suddenly into a thinner cloud, and the slightly increased light showed me something which made me clutch Juggins by the arm.

'"Hold hard!" I whispered as I squatted down. "What is that on the grave?"

'Juggins hauled out his six-shooter with a tug, and, looking at his face, I saw, what I had not noticed before, that he too was a trifle jumpy, though why I cannot say. He squatted down quietly enough by my side, and pressed up against me, a bit closer, I fancied, than he would have thought necessary at any other time. I whispered to Juggins telling him not to shoot, and we sat there for nearly a minute, I should think, peering through the darkness, trying to make out what was the black thing on the grave, that was making that scratching noise.

'Then the moon came out into a patch of open sky, and we saw clearly at last, and what it showed me did not make me feel better. The creature we had been looking at was kneeling on the grave facing us. It, or rather she, was an old, old Sâkai hag. She was stark naked, and in the clear moonlight I could see her long pendulous breasts, and the creases all over her withered old hide, which were wrinkles filled with dirt. Her hair hung about her face in great matted locks, falling forward as she bent above the grave, and her eyes glinted through the elf-locks like those of some unclean animal. Her long fingers, with nails like claws to them, were tearing at the dirt of the grave, and the exertion made her sweat so that her body shone in the moonlight.

'"Juggins," whispered I, "here is some one else who wants this precious baby of yours for a specimen."

'I felt him jump to his feet, but I clutched at him, and pulled him back.

'"Keep still, man!" I whispered. "Let us see what the old hag is doing. It is not the brat's mother, is it?"

'"No," whispered Juggins, "this is an older woman. What a ghoul it is!"

'Then we were silent again. Where we squatted we were hidden from the hag by a few tufts of rank *lâlang* grass, and the shadow from the jungle also covered us. Even if we had been in the open, I doubt whether that old woman would have seen us, she was so eagerly intent upon her work. For five minutes or more—I know it seemed an age to me at the time—we sat there watching her scrape, and tear, and scratch at the earth of the grave, and all the while her lips kept going like a shivering man's teeth, though no sound, that I could hear, came from them. At length she got down to the corpse, and I saw her draw the bark wrapper out of the grave, and take the baby's body out of it. Then she sat back on her heels, and threw her head up, just like a dog, and bayed at the moon. She did it three times, and I do not know what there was in the sound that jangled up one's nerves, but each time I heard it my hair fairly lifted. Then she laid the little body down in a position that seemed to have something to do with the points of the compass, for she took a long time arranging it before she was satisfied with the direction of its head and feet.

'Then she got up and began to dance round and round the grave. It was not a pretty sight, out there in the semi-darkness, and miles away from every one and everything, to watch this abominable old hag capering uncleanly, while those restless, noiseless lips of hers called upon all the devils in Hell, in words that we could not hear. Juggins pushed harder against me than ever, and his hand on my arm gripped tighter and tighter. I looked at his face, and saw that it was as white as chalk, and I daresay mine was not much better. It does not sound much, as I tell it to you here, in a civilised house, but at the time the sight of that weird figure dancing in the moonlight, with its ungainly shadow, fairly scared me.

'She danced silently like that for some minutes; setting to the dead baby, and to her own uncouth capering shadow, till the sight made me feel sick. If anybody had told me that morning, that I should ever be badly frightened by an old woman, I should have laughed; but I saw nothing to laugh at in the idea, while that grotesque dancing lasted.

'When it was over she squatted down again with her back towards us, and took up the baby. She nursed it as a mother might nurse her child. I could see the curve of the thing's head beyond her thin left arm, and its little legs dangled loosely near her right elbow. Then she began to croon to it, swinging it gently from side to side. She rocked it slowly at first, but gradually the pace quickened, until she was swaying her body to and fro, and from side to side, at such a pace, that to me she looked as though she was falling all ways at once. And all the time that queer crooning kept getting faster and faster, and more awful to listen to. Then suddenly she changed the motion. She seized the thing she was nursing by its arms, and began dancing it up and down, still moving at a fearful pace, and crooning worse than ever. I could see the little puckered face of the thing above her head, every time she danced it up, and then, as she danced it down again, I lost sight of it for a second, until it reappeared once more. I kept my eye fixed on the thing's face every time it came up, and—do not believe me if you had rather not—it began to be *alive*. Its eyes seemed to me to be open, and its mouth was working like a little child's when it tries to laugh and is too young to do it properly. Juggins saw it too, for I could hear him drawing his breath harder, and shorter than a healthy man should. Then, all in a moment, she did something. It looked to me as though she bent forward and kissed it, and at that very instant a cry went up like the wail of a lost soul. It may have been something in the jungle, but I know my jungles pretty thoroughly, and I swear to you that I have never heard any cry like it before or since. Then, before we knew what she was doing, that old hag threw the body back into the grave, and began dumping down the earth, and jumping on it, while the cry grew fainter and fainter. It all happened so quickly, that I had not time to think of doing anything, till I was startled back into action by the sharp crack of Juggin's pistol in my ear as he fired at the hag.

'"She's burying it alive!" cried Juggins, which was a queer thing for a man to say, who had seen the baby lying stark and dead more than thirty hours earlier, but the same thought was in my mind too, and we started forward at a run. The hag had vanished into the jungle like a shadow. Juggins had missed her, he was always a shocking bad shot, but we did not trouble about her. We just threw ourselves upon the grave, and dug at it with our hands until the baby lay in my arms. It was cold and stiff, and putrefaction had already begun its work. I forced open its mouth, and saw something that I expected. The tip of its tongue was missing. It had been bitten off by a set of very bad teeth, for the edge of it was like a saw.

'"The thing is quite dead," I said to Juggins.

'"But it cried! it cried!" sobbed Juggins, "I can hear it now. Oh to think that we let that hag kill it."

'Juggins sat down with his head in his hands. He was utterly unmanned. Now that the fright was over, I was beginning to be quite brave again. It is a way I have.

'"Never mind," I said. "Here is your specimen if you want it." I had put the thing down, and now pointed at it from a distance. It was not pleasant to touch. But Juggins only shuddered.

'"Bury it in Heaven's name!" he said. "I would not have it for all the world. Besides it *was* alive. I saw and heard it."'

'Well, we put it back in the grave, and next day we left the Sâkai country. We had seen quite as much of it as we wanted for a bit, I tell you.

'Juggins and I swore one another to secrecy, as neither of us fancied being told we were drunk or lying. You, however, know something of the uncanny things of the East, and to-night I have told the story to you. Now I am going to turn in. Do not give me away.'

Young Middleton went off to bed, and last year he died of fever and dysentery somewhere up country. His name was not Middleton, of course, so I am not really 'giving him away,' as he called it, even now. As for his companion, though he is still alive, I have called him Juggins, and, since the family is a large one, he will not, perhaps, be identified.

UP COUNTRY

> The days are hot and damp, and my legs are stiff with cramp,
>   And the office punkahs creak!
> And I'd give my tired soul, for the life that makes man whole,
>   And a whiff of the jungle reek!
> Ha' done with the tents of Shem, dear boys,
>   With office stool and pew,
> For it's time to turn to the lone Trail, our own Trail, the far Trail,
>   Dig out, dig out on the old trail—
>   The trail that is always new.
>
> A Parody.

IT has been said that a white man, who has lived twelve consecutive months in complete isolation, among the people of an alien Asiatic race, is never wholly sane again for the remainder of his days. This, in a measure, is true; for the life he then learns to live, and the discoveries he makes in that unmapped land, the gates of which are closed, locked, barred, and chained against all but a very few of his countrymen, teach him to love many things which all right-minded people very properly detest. The free, queer, utterly unconventional life has a fascination which is all its own. Each day brings a little added knowledge of the hopes and fears, longings and desires, joys and sorrows, pains and agonies of the people among whom his lot is cast. Each hour brings fresh insight into the mysterious workings of the minds and hearts of that very human section of our race, which ignorant Europeans calmly class as 'niggers.' All these things come to possess a charm for him, the power of which grows apace, and eats into the very marrow of the bones of the man who has once tasted this particular fruit of the great Tree of Knowledge. Just as the old smugglers, in the Isle of Man, were wont to hear the sea calling to them; go where he may, do what he will, the voice of the jungle, and of the people who dwell in those untrodden places, sounds in the ears of one who has lived the life. Ever and anon it cries to him to come back, come back to the scenes, the people, the life which he knows and understands, and which, in spite of all its hardships, he has learned to love.

The great wheel of progress, like some vast snowball, rolls steadily along, gathering to itself all manner of weird and unlikely places and people, filling up the hollows, laying the high hills low. Rays of searching garish light reflected from its surface are pitilessly flashed into the dark places of the earth, which have been wrapped around by the old-time dim religious light, since first the world began. The people in whose eyes these rays beat so mercilessly, reel and stumble blindly on in their march through life, taking wrong turnings at every step, and going woefully astray. Let us hope that succeeding generations will become used to the new conditions, and will fight their way back to a truer path; for there is no blinking the fact that the first, immediate, and obvious effects of our spirit of progress upon the weaker races, tend towards degeneration.

UP COUNTRY

Ten years ago the Peninsula was very different from what it has since become, and many places where the steam-engine now shrieks to the church bells, and the shirt-collar galls the perspiring neck, were but recently part and parcel of that vast 'up country,' which is so little known but to the few who dwell in it, curse it,—and love it.

> I sent my soul through the invisible,
> Some Letter of the After-Life to spell,
> And Presently my Soul returned to me
> And whispered 'Thou thyself art Heaven or Hell.

So sings the old Persian poet, lying in his rose garden, by the wine-cup that robbed him of his Robe of Honour, and his words are true; though not quite in the sense in which he wrote them. For this wisdom the far-away jungles also teach a man who has to rely solely upon himself, and upon his own resources, for the manner of his life, and the form which it is to take. To all dwellers in the desolate solitude, which every white man experiences, who is cast alone among natives, there are two 'up countries'—his Heaven and Hell, and both are of his own making. The latter is the one of which he speaks to his fellow race-mates— if he speaks at all about his solitary life. The former lies at the back of his heart, and is only known to himself, and then but dimly known till the time comes for a return to the Tents of Shem. Englishmen, above all other men, revel in their privilege of being allowed to grumble and 'grouse' over the lives which the Fates have allotted to them. They speak briefly, roughly, and gruffly of the hardships they endure, making but little of them perhaps, and talking as though their lives, as a matter of course, were made up of these things only. The instinct of the race is to see life through the national pea-soup fog, which makes all things dingy, unlovely, and ugly. Nothing is more difficult than to induce men of our race to confess that in their lives —hard though they may have been—good things have not held aloof, and that they have often been quite happy under the most unlikely circumstances, and in spite of the many horrors and privations which have long encompassed them about.

Let us take the Hell first. We often have to do so, making a virtue of necessity, and a habit is a habit; moreover, our pains are always more interesting than our pleasures—to our neighbours. Therefore, let us take the dark view of up-country life to start upon. In the beginning, when first a man turns from his own people, and dwells in isolation among an alien race, he suffers many things. The solitude of soul— that terrible solitude which is only to be experienced in a crowd—the dead monotony, without hope of change; the severance from all the pleasant things of life, and the want of any substitutes for them, eat into the heart and brain of him as a corrosive acid eats into iron. He longs for the fellowship of his own people with an exceeding great longing, till it becomes a burden too grievous to bear; he yearns to find comradeship among the people of the land, but he knows not yet the manner by which their confidence may be won, and they, on their side, know him for a stranger within their gates, view him with keen suspicion, and hold him at arm's length. His ideas, his prejudices, his modes of thought, his views on every conceivable subject differ too widely from their own, for immediate sympathy to be possible between him and them. His habits are the habits of a white man, and many little things, to which he has not yet learned to attach importance, are as revolting to the natives, as the pleasant custom of spitting on the carpet, which some old-world *Rajas* still affect, is to Europeans. His manners, too, from the native point of view, are as bad as his habits are unclean. He is respected for his wisdom, hated for his airs of superiority, pitied for his ignorance of many things, feared for what he represents, laughed at for his eccentric habits and customs, despised for his infidelity to the Faith, abhorred for his want of beauty, according to native standards of taste, and loved not at all. The men disguise their feelings, skilfully as only Orientals can, but the women and the little children do not scruple to show what their sentiments really are. When he goes abroad, the old women snarl at him as he passes, and spit ostentatiously, after the native manner when some unclean thing is at hand. The mothers snatch up their little ones and carry them hurriedly away, casting a look of hate and fear over their shoulders as they run. The children scream and yell, clutch their mothers' garments, or trip and fall, howling dismally the while, in their frantic efforts to fly his presence. He is Frankenstein's monster, yearning for love and fellowship with his kind, longing to feel the hand of a friend in his, and yet knowing, by the unmistakable signs which a sight of him causes, that he is indescribably repulsive to the people among whom he lives. Add to all this that he is cut off from all the things which, to educated Europeans, make life lovely, and you will realise that his is indeed a sorry case. The privations of the body, if he has sufficient grit to justify his existence, count for little. He can live on any kind of food, sleep on the hardest of hard mats, or on the bare ground, with his head and feet in a puddle, if needs must. He can turn night into day, and sleep through the sunlight, or sleep not at all, as the case may be, if any useful purpose is to be served thereby. These are not things to trouble him, though the fleshpots of Egypt are very good when duty allows him to turn his back for a space upon the desert. Privations all these things are called in ordinary parlance, but they are of little moment, and are good for his liver. The real privations are of quite another sort. He never hears music; never sees a lovely picture; never joins in the talk and listens lovingly to conversation which strikes the answering sparks from his sodden brain. Above all, he never encounters the softening influence of the society of ladies of his own race. His few books are for a while his companions, but he reads them through and through, and cons them o'er and o'er, till the best sayings of the best authors ring flat on his sated ears like the echo of a twice-told tale. He has not yet learned that there is a great and marvellous book lying beneath his hand, a book in which all may read if they find but the means of opening the clasp which locks it, a book in which a man may read for years and never know satiety, which, though older than the hills, is ever new, and which, though studied for a lifetime, is never exhausted, and is never completely understood.

This knowledge comes later; and it is then that the Chapter of the Great Book of Human Nature, which deals with natives, engrosses his attention and, touching the grayness of his life, like the rising sun, turns it into gold and purple.

Many other things he has to endure. Educated white men have inherited an infinite capacity for feeling bored; and a hot climate, which fries us all over a slow fire, grills boredom into irritability. The study of oriental human nature requires endless patience; and this is the hardest virtue for a young, energetic white man, with the irritable brain of his race, to acquire. Without it life is a misery—for

> It is not good for the Christian's health
>   To hurry the Aryan brown,
> For the Christian riles and the Aryan smiles,
>   And he weareth the Christian down;
> And the end of that fight is a tombstone white,
>   With the name of the late deceased,
> And the epitaph clear, A fool lies here
>   Who tried to hustle the East.

Then gradually, very gradually, and by how slow degrees he shudders in after days to recall, a change comes o'er the spirit of his nightmare. Almost unconsciously, he begins to perceive that he is sundered from the people of the land by a gulf which *they* can never hope to bridge over. If he is ever to gain their confidence the work must be of his own doing. They cannot come up to this level, he must go down to the plains in which they dwell. He must put off many of the things of the white man, must forget his airs of superiority, and must be content to be merely a native Chief among natives. His pride rebels, his prejudices cry out and will not be silenced, he knows that he will be misunderstood by his race-mates, should they see him among the people of his adoption, but the aching solitude beats down one and all of these things; and, like that eminently sensible man, the Prophet Muhammad, he gets him to the Mountain, since it is immovable and will not come to him.

Then begins a new life. He must start by learning the language of his fellows, as perfectly as it is given to a stranger to learn it. That is but the first step in a long and often a weary march. Next, he must study, with the eagerness of Browning's Grammarian, every native custom, every native conventionality, every one of the ten thousand ceremonial observances to which natives attach so vast an importance. He must grow to understand each one of the hints and *doubles ententes*, of which Malays make such frequent use, every little mannerism, sign and token, and, most difficult of all, every motion of the hearts, and every turn of thought, of those whom he is beginning to call his own people. He must become conscious of native Public Opinion, which is often diametrically opposed to the opinion of his race-mates on one and the same subject. He must be able to unerringly predict how the slightest of his actions will be regarded by the natives, and he must shape his course accordingly, if he is to maintain his influence with them, and to win their sympathy and their confidence. He must be able to place himself in imagination in all manner of unlikely places, and thence to instinctively feel the native Point of View. That is really the whole secret of governing natives. A quick perception of their Point of View, under all conceivable circumstances, a rapid process by which a European places himself in the position of the native, with whom he is dealing, an instinctive and instantaneous apprehension of the precise manner in which he will be affected, and a clear vision of the man, his feelings, his surroundings, his hopes, his desires, and his sorrows,—these, and these alone, mean that complete sympathy, without which the white man among Malays, is but as a sounding brass and as a tinkling cymbal.

It does not all come at once. Months, perhaps years, pass before the exile begins to feel that he is getting any grip upon the natives, and even when he thinks that he knows as much about them as is good for any man, the oriental soul shakes itself in its brown casing, and comes out in some totally unexpected and unlooked-for place, to his no small mortification and discouragement. But, when he has got thus far, discouragement matters little, for he has become bitten with the love of his discoveries, and he can no more quit them than the dipsomaniac can abandon the drams which are killing him.

Then he gets deep into a groove and is happy. His fingers are between the leaves of the Book of Human Nature, and his eager eyes are scanning the lines of the chapter which in time he hopes to make his own. The advent of another white man is a weariness of the flesh. The natives about him have learned to look upon him as one of their own people. His speech is their speech, he can think as they do, can feel as they feel, rejoice in their joys, and sorrow in their pains. He can tell them wonderful things, and a philosophy of which they had not dreamed. He never offends their susceptibilities, never wounds their self-respect, never sins against their numerous conventionalities. He has feasted with them at their weddings, doctored their pains, healed their sick, protected them from oppression, stood their friend in time of need, done them a thousand kindnesses, and has helped their dying through the strait and awful pass of death. Above all, he *understands*, and, in a manner, they love him. A new white man, speaking to him in an unknown tongue, seems to lift him for the time out of their lives. The stranger jars on the natives, who are the exile's people, and he, looking through the native eyes which are no longer strange to him, sees where his race-mate offends, and in his turn is jarred, until he begins to hate his own countrymen. Coming out of the groove hurts badly, and going back into it is almost worse, but when a man is once well set in the rut of native life, these do not disturb him, for he is happy, and has no need of other and higher things. This is the exile's Heaven.

As years go on the up-country life of which I write will become less and less common in this Peninsula of ours, and the Malays will be governed wholly by men, who, never having lived their lives, cannot expect to have more than a surface knowledge of the people whose destinies are in their hands. The Native States will, I fancy, be none the better governed, and those who rule them will miss much which has tended to widen the lives of the men who came before them, and who dwelt among the people while they were still as God made them.

And those who led these lives? The years will dim the memories of all they once learned and knew and experienced; and as they indite the caustic minute to the suffering subordinate, and strangle with swaddlings of red-tape the tender babe of prosperity, they will perchance look back with wonder at the men they once were, and thinking of their experiences in the days of long ago will marvel that each one of them as he left the desert experienced the pang of Chillon's prisoner :—

> Even I
> Regained my freedom with a sigh.

L'ENVOI

By the green shade of the palm trees,
    Where the river flows along
To be wedded to the calm seas,
    Dwell the people of my song.
With a languid step they wander
    Thro' the forest or the grove,
And with listless eyes they ponder
    On the glories poets love.
They have little joy in beauty,
    Little joy in virtue high,
Honour, mercy, truth, and duty,
    Or the creeds for which men die.
But their lives are calm and peaceful,
    And they ask for nothing more
Save some happy, listless, easeful
    Years, and peace from strife and war.

Tales I tell of women wailing,
  Cruel wrong and bitter strife,
Shrieking souls that pass, and quailing
  Hearts that shrink beneath the knife.
Tales I tell of evil passions,
  Men that suffer, men that slay,
All the tragedy that fashions
  Life and death for such as they.
Yet these things are but as fleeting
  Shadows, that more lightly pass
Than the sunlight, which retreating
  Leaves no stain upon the grass.
O my friends! I judge ye lightly,
  Listen to the tales I tell.
Answer, have I spoken rightly?
  Judge me, have I loved ye well?

THE END

Printed by R. & R. CLARK, LIMITED, *Edinburgh.*

www.ingramcontent.com/pod-product-compliance
Lightning Source LLC
Chambersburg PA
CBHW032135230426
43672CB00011B/2340